Anonymus

General Prisons Board (Ireland)

Eighteenth report, 1895-96, with appendix

Anonymus

General Prisons Board (Ireland)
Eighteenth report, 1895-96, with appendix

ISBN/EAN: 9783742810199

Manufactured in Europe, USA, Canada, Australia, Japa

Cover: Foto ©ninafisch / pixelio.de

Manufactured and distributed by brebook publishing software
(www.brebook.com)

Anonymus

General Prisons Board (Ireland)

EIGHTEENTH REPORT

OF THE

GENERAL PRISONS BOARD, IRELAND,

1895-96;

WITH AN APPENDIX.

Presented to both Houses of Parliament by Command of Her Majesty.

DUBLIN:
PRINTED FOR HER MAJESTY'S STATIONERY OFFICE,
BY ALEXANDER THOM & CO. (LIMITED).

And to be purchased, either directly or through any Bookseller, from
HODGES, FIGGIS, & CO. (LIMITED), 104, Grafton-street, Dublin; or
EYRE & SPOTTISWOODE, East Harding-street, Fleet-street, E.C.; or
JOHN MENZIES & CO., 12, Hanover-street, Edinburgh; and
90, West Nile-street, Glasgow.

1896.

[C.—8252.] *Price 7d.*

Dublin Castle,

8th August, 1896.

Sir,

I have to acknowledge the receipt of your letter of the 6th instant, forwarding, for submission to His Excellency the Lord Lieutenant, the Eighteenth Report of the General Prisons Board, Ireland, 1895-96.

I am,

Sir,

Your obedient servant,

D. Harrel.

The Chairman,

General Prisons Board,

Dublin Castle.

CONTENTS.

APPENDIX.

PART I.

PART II.—LOCAL PRISONS.

PART III.—CONVICT PRISONS.

CONTENTS.

PART IV.—REGISTRATION OF CRIMINALS.

PART V.—EXPENDITURE.—LOCAL AND CONVICT PRISONS.

EIGHTEENTH REPORT

OF THE

GENERAL PRISONS BOARD, IRELAND.

TO HIS EXCELLENCY GEORGE HENRY,
EARL CADOGAN, K.G.,

LORD LIEUTENANT GENERAL AND GENERAL GOVERNOR OF IRELAND.

General Prisons Board,
Dublin Castle,
29th July, 1896.

MAY IT PLEASE YOUR EXCELLENCY,

1. We have the honour, pursuant to statute, to present this our Eighteenth Annual Report on the condition of the prisons and prisoners within our jurisdiction, and with respect to the registration of criminals.

2. In accordance with the decision of Government, the principle adopted in the preparation of the Judicial Statistics, of having all tables with the exception of those relating to finance drawn up for the calendar year, has been followed in regard to the tables in the Appendix to this Report, which, with the exception mentioned, have been compiled likewise for the year ending 31st December, instead of for that ending 31st March, as for many years past was the case. Owing to this change, the figures for the first three months of 1895 which were included in the statistical tables printed with last year's report are again included in many of the tables now published. Statistics.

I.—LOCAL PRISONS.

3. Queenstown Bridewell was closed on 31st May, 1895. Of the 95 Bridewells which were in existence when the Prisons were handed over to the Board under the Act of 1877, all but 15 have been closed. Bridewells.

4. We are happy to state that the gradual reduction in the total number of committals to local prisons still continues, as appears from the following Table of committals to local prisons:— Committals.

COMMITMENTS, &c., exclusive of Committals under Civil Process.

Years.	Number of Committals.	Daily Average No. of Prisoners.	Proportion of Daily Average to 100,000 of estimated population.	Years.	Number of Committals.	Daily Average No. of Prisoners.	Proportion of Daily Average to 100,000 of estimated population.
1854, .	69,445	5,700	83	1883–84	45,781	2,680	54
1858, .	48,446	4,418	73	1884–85	37,829	2,678	52
1860, .	30,713	3,573	43	1885–86	39,884	2,601	53
1865, .	32,731	2,716	46	1886–87	40,764	2,643	54
1870, .	33,370	2,877	42	1887–88	40,779	2,666	53
1875, .	38,929	2,741	52	1888–89	43,704	2,648	55
1876, .	41,817	2,836	53	1889–90	44,793	2,646	53
1877, .	43,641	2,926	56	1890–91	40,765	2,605	55
1878–79	45,897	2,825	53	1891–92	37,868	2,497	53
1879–80	44,889	3,013	53	1892–93	34,365	2,316	50
1880–81	40,103	2,620	50	1893–94	34,187	2,488	53
1881–82	41,686	3,111	60	1894–95	31,474	2,517	50
1882–83	45,434	3,025	59	1895, .	30,270	2,135	47

B

Conduct of Prisoners.

5. The conduct of the prisoners has been satisfactory.

The following return gives the particulars and percentages of prisoners punished for the last five years :—

Year.	No. of Prison Offences.	No. of Prisoners punished.	Percentage of Prisoners punished to total number of Prisoners.
1891-2, ...	10,[illegible]	5,118	[illegible]
1892-3, ...	10,[illegible]	5,228	[illegible]
1893-4, ...	8,160	4,840	[illegible]
1894-5, ...	7,[illegible]	3,957	[illegible]
1895, ...	4,625	3,310	[illegible]

Short sentences.

6. From Table V. it will be seen that of the 26,034 commitments on conviction (excluding court-martial prisoners), 11,535, or 44 per cent., were for terms not exceeding a week; 4,899 or 19 per cent. for terms exceeding a week but not exceeding a fortnight; and 3,368, or 13 per cent., for terms exceeding a fortnight but not exceeding four weeks, while only 24 per cent. were for terms exceeding four weeks. About 50 per cent. of the convicted prisoners committed during the year were drunkards.

Juveniles.

7. From the following table it will be seen that a large diminution has taken place of late years in the number of convicted juvenile prisoners.

Return of Convicted Juveniles committed in following years.

Years.	Under 16 Years of age.		16 to 18 Years of age.		Total.		
	Boys.	Girls.	Boys.	Girls.	Boys.	Girls.	Boys & Girls.
1889-90, .	63	4	330	66	393	70	463
1890-91, .	44	8	337	63	381	71	[illegible]
1891-92, .	53	–	314	65	367	63	[illegible]
1892-93, .	59	3	275	73	334	75	[illegible]
1893-94, .	57	4	250	61	307	65	372
1894-95, .	25	3	218	56	243	59	302
1895, . .	30	–	207	30	237	30	267

Prison mortality.

8. It is again our duty to report a rate of mortality which is exceptionally low even for prison statistics. While the average daily number of prisoners in the local prisons during the year was 2,164, the number of deaths, excluding 1 execution, was 3; representing a death rate of 1·38 per thousand on the daily average number in custody. No doubt the mortality is much reduced by the number of prisoners who are released for medical reasons.

9. Subjoined is a table of mortality among prisoners for each year during the last sixteen years:—

Year.	Daily Average Number of Prisoners.	No. of Deaths.	Rate per Thousand	Year.	Daily Average Number of Prisoners.	No. of Deaths.	Rate per Thousand.
1880-1, .	2,629	14	5·34	1888-9, .	2,616	6	2·27
1881-2, .	3,111	16	5·78	1889-90, .	2,540	14	5·5
1882-3, .	3,693	7	2·31	1890-1, .	2,619	3	1·15
1883-4, .	2,697	11	4·08	1891-2, .	2,484	9	3·6
1884-5, .	2,572	10	3·76	1892-3, .	2,321	11	4·74
1885-6, .	2,801	16	5·34	1893-4, .	2,456	13	5·29
1886-7, .	2,843	8	2·80	1894-5, .	2,253	6	2·66
1887-8, .	2,469	12	5·07	1895, .	2,164	3	1·39

The causes of the three deaths were puerperal fever, cardiac asthma, and exhaustion following delirium tremens.

10. There was no case of either typhus or typhoid fever. Health of Prisoners.

11. Fifty-four prisoners were released on medical grounds during the year. Of the 54 there were 20 women who were near their confinement, and of the remaining 25 there were 23 cases of disease which were reported as having originated before reception.

12. The number of prisoners transferred as insane to asylums was seventy-five, of whom, on admission, sixty-one were reported to be insane, one weak-minded, and one doubtful. Of the remaining twelve there were four who were sane while in prison, but who were found to have been insane at the time when their offences were committed. Eight, therefore, became insane in prison, one of them three and another twelve days after committal. Lunacy

13. A change has been made in the regulations regarding the issue of secular books from the prison libraries to convicted prisoners. Secular Books.

Previous to May, 1895, no secular book was issued during the first month of imprisonment, and when one was issued it could not be changed for the next two months. Now all well-conducted and industrious prisoners are eligible to receive a secular book, which can be changed at the discretion of the Governor.

14. The following return shows the number of visits paid to the different prisons by the members of the Visiting Committees during the year :—

RETURN—MEETINGS OF VISITING COMMITTEES, 1895.

PRISONS.	Number of Meetings at which a quorum was present.	Number of Visits paid by individual Members.	PRISONS.	Number of Meetings at which a quorum was present.	Number of Visits paid by individual Members.
LARGER PRISONS.			LARGER PRISONS—*continued.*		
Armagh, . . .	14	2	Mountjoy, . . .	11	27
Belfast, . . .	4	9	Sligo, . . .	9	6
Castlebar, . . .	–	9	Tralee, . . .	9	6
Clonmel, . . .	8	14	Tullamore, . .	7	10
Cork, Male, . .	13	7	Waterford, . .	8	16
Cork, Female, . .	7	–	Wexford, . .	18	19
Dundalk, . . .	1	8			
Galway, . . .	8	8	MINOR PRISONS.		
Grangegorman, . .	10	14	Carrick-on-Shannon,	–	27
Killarney, . . .	6	9	Drogheda, . .	–	
Kilmainham, . .	5	9	Enniskillen, . .	–	–
Limerick, Male, . .	2	16	Mullingar, . .	1	1
Limerick, Female, .	6	7	Omagh, . . .	6	4
Londonderry, . .	11	1	Wicklow, . .	3	1

The Board desire again to express their acknowledgment of the valuable assistance rendered by Visiting Committees.

II.—CONVICT PRISONS.

15. The number of convicts in custody on 31st December, 1895, was :—

—	Male.	Female.	Total.
In Convict Prisons, . . .	384	30	414
In Local Prisons, . . .	15	–	15
Gross total of Convicts in Custody on 31st Dec., 1895, .	399	30	429

16. The number of convicts sentenced to penal servitude during the year ending 31st December, 1895, was:— New convictions.

—	Males.	Females.	Total.
5 years,	50	7	57
4 ,,	4	–	4
6 ,,	21	5	26
7 ,,	6	–	6
10 ,,	1	–	1
12 ,,	1	–	1
15 ,,	1	–	1
20 ,,	3	–	3
Life,	2	–	2
Death, commuted to P.S. for Life,	–	1	1
Gross Total sentenced during year,	89	13	102

17. Disposal of convicts during the year ending 31st December, 1895:— Convicts discharged.

—	Males.	Females.	Total.
Discharged from Prisons:—			
On Completion of Sentence,	3	–	3
On Commutation of Sentence,	4	1	5
On Licence,	131	17	148
Gross total disposed of during year,	138	18	154

18. The Revocations and Forfeitures of Licences in Ireland during the year ended 31st December, 1895, were as follow:— Revocation of Licences.

—	Males.	Females.	Total.
Forfeited for breach of conditions of Licence,	8	–	8
Forfeited or revoked in consequence of a conviction for other offences,	24	5	29
Gross Total,	32	5	37*

* Two of these were English Licence holders.

19. The following table shows the number of convicts convicted, discharged, and in custody at intervals of five years between 1854 and 1880–1, and for every successive year to the present time:—

TABLE showing the number of Convicts "Convicted," "Discharged," and in "Custody," in certain years since the year 1854 inclusive.

Year.	No. Convicted.	No. Discharged.*	In custody on January 1st.		
	M. and F.	M. and F.	M.	F.	Total.
1854	710	658	–	–	†3,488
1855	518	880	3,067	430	3,497
1860	331	524	1,187	444	1,631
1865	299	410	1,272	504	1,776
1870	248	253	878	342	1,220
1875	241	229	852	281	1,133
1880–81	123	311	669	168	837
1881–82	209	218	694	110	804
1882–83	200	161	793	105	898
1883–84	145	161	782	88	870
1884–85	137	184	754	82	836
1885–86	79	197	700	66	766
1886–87	87	248	566	66	632
1887–88	102	163	524	54	578
1888–89	77	155	472	46	518
1889–90	83	104	426	28	454
1890–91	86	176	436	26	462
1891–92	125	117	443	37	480
1892–93	96	118	441	30	471
1893–94	108	103	446	39	485
1894–95	115	147	437	27	464
1895	107	154	427	27	454

* Including those discharged after forfeiture or revocation of licenses.
† In addition to this number there were 345 convicts under detention in the county prisons, and several hundreds in Bermuda and Gibraltar, who were subsequently discharged in Ireland.

20. The conduct of the Convicts has been generally good. There was no case of corporal punishment.

The following return gives the particulars and percentages of Convicts punished for the last five years:—

Year.	No. of Prison Offences.	No. of Prisoners punished.	Per-centage of Prisoners punished to Total Number of Prisoners.
1891–92, ...	431	130	[illegible]
1892–93, ...	373	140	[illegible]
1893–94, ...	453	168	[illegible]
1894–95, ...	435	146	33·79
1895, ...	404	146	27·11

21. In the convict prisons there were five deaths; two of these were caused by apoplexy, the others by hepatitis, cardiac failure, and laryngitis. *Health of Convicts.*

There were no cases of either typhus or typhoid fever.

Fourteen were released on medical grounds, and ten were transferred to the Criminal Lunatic Asylum.

III.—GENERAL.

22. In June and July, 1895, the Quinquennial International Penitentiary Congress was held in Paris, and was attended by the Chairmen of the English, Scotch, and Irish Prisons Boards, the first-mentioned officially representing the English Government. *International Congress.*

23. The regulations for the recruiting of warders for the service have been altered. The supply of candidates being far in excess of the requirements, the standard of height for ordinary warders has been raised from 5 feet 6 inches to 5 feet 8 inches, while the limit of age has (with certain exceptions) been reduced from 31 to 30 years, the standard of the literary examination being also somewhat raised. *Candidates.*

24. In order to lessen the hours of duty of warders and to relieve them, as far as possible, from the extra evening duty which they have been liable to perform, the Board represented to the Government that it was desirable the staff should be increased, and they are glad to report that the Treasury have sanctioned an increase of 24 ordinary warders and 8 assistant matrons to the staff of the Irish Prisons. *Prison Staff.*

25. During the year the Board obtained the approval of the Government for an important alteration in their male officers' uniform, by the supply of a serge jacket and trousers for use in summer instead of the heavy cloth tunic and trousers hitherto in wear all the year round. This change was introduced on 1st May, 1896, and the Board are aware that it has greatly conduced to the comfort of their staff. *Uniform.*

26. The profit in the Manufacturing Department during 1895–6 amounted to £8,829 12s. 1d. This shows a falling off of £210 3s. 1d. as compared with the year 1894–5, which is sufficiently accounted for by the decrease in the number of prisoners. For some years no absolutely non-productive employment, such as the crank or treadmill, has been used in Irish prisons, and oakum picking has greatly diminished during the past year. Stone-breaking and mat-making have been increased, the former industry having been introduced during the year into Waterford Prison, and the latter into Galway, Kilkenny, and Londonderry Prisons. *Industries.*

27. In certain prisons carpet beating was one of the employments for prisoners. It was very profitable, but grave objections existed to it on the grounds of the association of prisoners which it entailed, and the risk of introducing infection into the prison. This form of employment has therefore been discontinued, and more suitable industries substituted.

28. A considerable amount of work is done in the prisons for Government Departments, such as firewood cutting for the Board of Works and War Department, washing for the Royal Irish Constabulary, Metropolitan Police, and War Department, mat-making for the Board of Public Works, and the manufacture of mail bags for the Irish Postal Service.

29. The warders' cottages referred to in last year's report in connection with Mountjoy Prison have been completed, and are now occupied. Warders' cottages are in course of erection at Armagh and Galway. The work of reconstruction at Cork Prison, which is being carried out by convicts transferred from Mountjoy, has been considerably advanced during the year, and will continue to furnish employment for a party of convicts for the next year.

30. The important question of the best form of labour for prisoners is one to which much attention has been directed of late. The International Penitentiary Congress referred to above, considered agricultural labour as the best from a reformatory point of view, and the Departmental Committee on Prisons in England, 1895, reported as follows on the subject, namely, para. 64:—

"We regret very much that there is not more opportunity for work in gardens or on the land. It is agreed by all medical experts and prison officials that no kind of employment is more useful. It is healthy, productive, varied, and of a more or less interesting character. Plain hard digging may, under suitable conditions, be found a valuable and wholesome substitute for hard labour, while the lighter forms of field and garden work would be adapted for other cases."

31. As the small quantity of land attached to the only two Male Convict Prisons now in Ireland, viz., Mountjoy (Dublin), and Maryboro', did not furnish sufficient field for the occupation of more than a very few of the convicts at agricultural labour, a farm of land containing about 34 acres, adjoining Maryboro' Prison, has been purchased for this purpose, and 51 convicts have already been transferred there from Mountjoy Prison.

32. It is proposed that the convicts removed from time to time from Mountjoy shall be generally taken from the select division (first offenders), and others offering best hopes of reformation. There would still remain at Mountjoy the convicts in probation and the worst class of habitual offenders, with others better suited for sedentary employment.

33. The Board hope the removal of a number of convicts from Mountjoy, and their employment on the land at Maryboro', will considerably lessen, if not entirely remove, an admitted defect in the Irish prison system, i.e., the concentration of a large body of convicts in a city, to which the Royal Commission of 1884 called attention.

34. As regards the other prisons a considerably increased area has recently been brought under cultivation at Belfast, Grangegorman, Kilkenny, and Tralee Prisons, and now all available ground at the various local prisons is tilled by prison labour.

35. Two additional Prisoners' Aid Societies have been established—one at Limerick, the other at Belfast. The former has been certified under the Prisons Act, and an application from the other for a certificate is at present before the Government. The Board are glad to notice a tendency to increase these philanthropic and useful institutions. Prisoners' Aid Societies.

The following are the existing certified Societies :—

DUBLIN :

Roman Catholic Female Prisoners' Aid Society.
Roman Catholic Male Prisoners' Aid Society.
Society for the Relief of Poor Protestants (Male and Female) discharged from Prison.

BELFAST :

Prison Gate Mission for Women (Protestant).
Prison Gate Mission for Men (Protestant).

LIMERICK.

Limerick Prisoners' Aid Society (undenominational).

IV.—REGISTRATION OF CRIMINALS.

36. The Board, in their last report, referred to the anthropometric system of identifying criminals as about to be put in force in this country. They pointed out at the same time, that though they would have preferred to have adopted the French or Bertillon system in its entirety as being completely successful, they proposed to follow the modification of the system recommended by the Committee, and adopted in England; for if the descriptive particulars of criminals in Ireland were not made out in the same form as in Great Britain, the practical value of the system would be obviously impaired. Anthropometry.

37. It having been in consequence decided that the English system should be adopted, a class of prison officers from different prisons was instructed for several days, in April of present year, at Mountjoy Prison in the method of taking the various measurements, &c., by Dr. J. G. Garson, of the Anthropometric Department, Scotland Yard, London, and this system of measurement has been adopted at six prisons, as a beginning, for a certain class of prisoners.

V.—DEPARTMENTAL.

38. The Board regret to have to record the death of their Architect, Mr. William J. Welland, C.E.; also of Mr. John Brennan, Clerk in the Habitual Criminal Registry; and Mr. Michael Hand, Agent for Discharged Prisoners.

39. Mr. A. J. Hamilton Smythe, M.Inst.C.E., has been appointed Engineering Inspector in the place of Mr. Welland; Mr. Brennan's place has been filled by the transfer of Mr. Henry Chamney from the Store Division; and Mr. John Bolton has been appointed temporarily as Agent for Discharged Prisoners.

VI.—APPENDIX.

40. We beg to refer to the Appendix for Copies of Circulars, Tabular Returns, and Official Reports.

We have the honour to be

Your Excellency's obedient Servants,

J. S. GIBBONS, *Chairman.*

JOHN MULHALL, *Vice-Chairman.*

STEWART WOODHOUSE, M.A., M.D.

APPENDIX

TO

EIGHTEENTH REPORT OF THE GENERAL PRISONS BOARD.

PART I.

CIRCULARS AND CIRCULAR MEMORANDA.

4,326/95.

Circular No. 432.

General Prisons Board, Dublin Castle,
29th April, 1895.

The Governors (or other Officers in charge) of H.M. Prisons.

I am directed by the General Prisons Board to instruct you that local prisoners who are treated in hospital, or exempted from labour, by order of the Medical Officer, are to be credited with the usual number of marks during the time they are so treated or exempted, if their conduct is good.

So much therefore of Circular 246 as requires such cases to be specially submitted for the consideration of the Board is hereby cancelled (4,326).

By order,
S. H. Douglas, Secretary.

Circular No. 433.

General Prisons Board, Dublin Castle,
11th May, 1895.

To the Governors of H.M. Local Prisons.

I am directed by the General Prisons Board to forward, and beg to enclose herewith, a copy of revised Classification and Labour Tables which are to come into force at once.

Printed copies for posting up in cells will be issued subsequently.

All industrious and well-conducted prisoners are now eligible to receive one secular book at a time, to be changed at the discretion of the Governor (4,968).

By order,
S. H. Douglas, Secretary.

4,849/95.

Circular No. 434.

General Prisons Board, Dublin Castle,
16th May, 1895.

To the Governors (or other Officers in charge) of H.M. Local Prisons.

In continuation of the directions in Circular 432, I am to further instruct you that marks granted to well-conducted prisoners while in hospital, or exempted from labour by order of the Medical Officer, are to count for gratuity in the same manner as marks earned in the usual way.

By order,
S. H. Douglas, Secretary.

Circular No. 435.

General Prisons Board, Dublin Castle,
14th June, 1895.

To the Governors (or other Officers in charge) of H.M. Local Prisons.

I am directed to state, for your information and guidance, that Circular No. 90, relative to the beds of Convicts during the period of their detention in Local Prisons while awaiting transfer to a Convict Prison, is cancelled, and that, in future, Convicts, while in a Local Prison, shall be treated as in a Convict Prison, by being supplied with a mattress (6,458).

By order,
S. H. Douglas, Secretary.

Circular No. 437.

General Prisons Board, Dublin Castle,
15th October, 1895.

To the Governors (or other Officers in charge) of H.M. Prisons.

When a prisoner who has been transferred to your custody from Dundrum Central Lunatic Asylum is about to be discharged from Prison, please notify the date of discharge, if possible a week beforehand, to the Resident Medical Superintendent of Dundrum Asylum, and in the event of any such prisoner dying in Prison, inform the Resident Medical Superintendent of the fact of the prisoner's death (11,031).

By order,
S. H. Douglas, Secretary.

Circular No. 439.

General Prisons Board, Dublin Castle,
19th November, 1895.

To the Governors (or other Officers in charge) of H.M. Local Prisons.

I am directed to forward, for your information and guidance, the following order of the General Prisons Board, respecting letters and visits of Local prisoners, viz.:—

Governors are authorised to allow any prisoner who is entitled to a visit to write a letter and to receive a reply in lieu of such visit, should his friends be unable to visit him.

They are also authorised to allow any prisoner to write a special letter, and to receive a reply under any of the following circumstances, if in their judgment it is desirable:—

(a.) The death of a near relative.
(b.) To give instructions as to his business or family affairs of an urgent nature.
(c.) To make arrangements for obtaining employment or assistance from friends on release (13,106).

By order,
S. H. Douglas, Secretary.

Circular No. 440.

General Prisons Board, Dublin Castle,
22nd November, 1895.

To the Governors (or other Officers in charge) of H.M. Prisons.

The General Prisons Board wish to remind Medical Officers that they may, on their own responsibility, without waiting for the sanction of the Board, call in an external trained nurse in urgent cases of dangerous illness, midwifery cases, &c., when, in their opinion, the attendance of the Hospital Warder or Matron would be insufficient. Each such case is to be immediately reported to the Board (13,168).

By order,
S. H. Douglas, Secretary.

Circular No. 441.

General Prisons Board, Dublin Castle,
29th November, 1895.

To the Governors of H.M. Prisons.

I am directed by the General Prisons Board to inform you that they have received the sanction of His Excellency the Lord Lieutenant for certain changes in the system of the issue of uniform to the male officers of the Irish Prisons Service.

The issues at present are:—

1 cap annually,
1 cloth tunic annually,
1 pair trousers every eight months,
1 great coat biennially,
2 pair boots annually.

The new issues, which are to be general, and to take place on fixed dates, are as follows:—

1 cap annually,
1 cloth tunic biennially,
1 pair cloth trousers annually,
1 summer jacket annually,
1 pair summer trousers annually,
1 great coat triennially,
2 pair boots annually.

The principal change consists in the supply of a light jacket and trousers for use in summer instead of the present cloth garments, and the Board are of opinion that this change will conduce greatly to the comfort of their Staff. It is intended that the new summer clothing, with boots, shall be supplied on 1st April next to all officers, and that cloth uniform of an improved pattern and boots shall be issued to all officers on 1st October next. Preparatory to these changes it is meanwhile necessary to order that no cloth uniform clothing or boots due under present arrangements between 1st January, 1896, and 30th September, 1896, shall be supplied. As regards caps, those officers entitled under present arrangements to a cap between 1st January, 1896, and 31st March, 1896, will be supplied on 1st April, 1896, and those entitled to one after 31st March, 1896, will be supplied on 1st October,

1896. As regards great coats, those officers becoming due for a great coat under present arrangements between 1st January, 1896, and 30th September, 1896, will get a new coat on 1st October, 1896; others becoming due between 1st October, 1896, and 30th September, 1897, will get a new coat on 1st October, 1897, and any becoming due after that date will be supplied on 1st October, 1898.

The issue of serge trousers to Trade Warders and Vanmen will be discontinued on 31st December 1895. Such officers will be allowed a working jacket, together with linen overall trousers, but the overalls are to form part of the floating stock of the prison, and the working jackets are not on any pretext to be worn by the officers when off duty. Any Trade Warders, or Warders acting as Vanmen, or Storekeepers, becoming due for a jacket under present arrangements between 1st January, 1896, and 31st March, 1896, will get it at the same time as hitherto, and any becoming due after 31st March, 1896, will not be supplied until 1st October, 1896, when all such officers will be supplied with a working jacket of a new shape.

Detailed regulations on the subject of the uniforms will be shortly issued. The Board expect that those officers who, under the old arrangements would become entitled to any article of uniform between 1st January next and the date of issue of the new uniform, will do their utmost to keep their present uniform neat and tidy during the additional period required of it, and Governors of the Prisons should endeavour to reduce any temporary inconvenience in such cases by having the necessary repairs to the uniforms promptly and neatly executed. In exceptional cases applications from officers for part worn clothing will be considered.

By order,

E. Metcalfe,

Superintendent of Stores.

Circular No. 442.

General Prisons Board, Dublin Castle,

6th December, 1895.

To the Governors of H.M. Local Prisons.

With reference to the directions in Circular 50 as to the report to be made in every case of the committal to your custody of a prisoner who, having been found by a jury to be of unsound mind and not capable of pleading, or having been acquitted upon the ground of insanity, has been ordered by the Court to be detained in custody during the pleasure of the Lord Lieutenant, I am directed to request that you will, in each such case in future, forward, for the information of the Inspectors of Lunatics, a detailed report from the Medical Officer (such as that referred to in Circular 318), giving a short history of the case, and of the opinion he has formed of it from personal observation, with a statement as to the treatment adopted by him during the lunatic's confinement in Prison (13,500).

By order,

S. H. Douglas, Secretary.

Circular No. 443.

General Prisons Board, Dublin Castle,
12th December, 1895.

To the Governors (or other Officers in charge) of H.M. Prisons.

In future every injury that a Prison Officer may receive is to be noted in the Governor's Journal.

If the injury is of a serious character, or likely to permanently affect the health or condition of the injured officer, or eventually to disable the officer for further service, a full record of the date and nature of the injury and of the circumstances under which it was sustained, with the names of the witnesses and a copy of the report of the Medical Officer, is to be drawn up and submitted to the Board, and, when received back, is to be entered in the form approved in the Officers' Conduct Book. A short record of the injury should also be made in the observation column of the Officer's Conduct Sheet, as well as in the Governor's Journal. The Medical Officer's report should include the general state of health and physical condition of the officer at the time when the injury was sustained.

It is desirable that, if possible, the record should contain such information as will enable it to be decided whether the person was injured (*a*) in the actual discharge of his duty, (*b*) without his own default, and (*c*) by some injury specifically attributable to the nature of his duty.

Without such proofs of injuries, claims for special gratuity or pensions in consequence will not be entertained. Should any officer, therefore, who has received a serious injury have any doubt of its being registered, he will be allowed, if he desires it, to see and sign the entry in the Conduct Book at the time, or as soon after, as, from the state of his injuries, he may be able, and the Governors will furnish officers so injured with a copy of the entry made in the Conduct Book, if desired (13,956).

By order,

S. H. Douglas, Secretary.

Circular No. 444.

General Prisons Board, Dublin Castle,
12th December, 1895.

To the Sub-Accounting Officer of each Prison.

The General Prisons Board has to impress upon you, that as Sub-Accounting Officer, you are responsible for all receipts and payments of money in respect of the Prison under your charge, or of the Minor Prisons or Bridewells (if any) for which you account; and that although in your absence and for your convenience Imprests are made payable to the Prison Officer who may be acting for you, you are responsible and accountable for the Imprests.

The Board desire further to inform you that it is your duty as the Sub-Accounting Officer to make all payments personally, and should you in any instance intrust this duty to another Prison Officer, it will be on your own responsibility.

To prevent misapprehension you are informed that the first paragraph on page 17 of "Preliminary Instructions," in reference to system of Store Accounts, does not at present apply to any Prison in Ireland—Circular 171, dated 26th June, 1880, is hereby cancelled, its purport being embodied in this Circular (13,978).

By order of the Board,

R. Lewis,
Clerk in charge of Accounts.

The ——

—— Prison.

Circular No. 446
(as amended on 10th March, 1898).

General Prisons Board, Dublin Castle,
26th February, 1896.

To the Governors (or other Officers in charge) of H.M. Local Prisons.

I am directed to request that you will report to the General Prisons Board the case of every person committed to the prison under your charge as a vagrant, or an offender against the laws in force for the relief of the destitute poor, who has four shillings or upwards in cash in possession, with a view to its being decided whether any, and, if so, how much, of such money shall be forfeited, and applied towards the payment of the expense of maintenance of such person in prison under the 39th Section of the Act, 19 and 20 Vic., c. 68.

The report, which is to be accompanied by the prisoner's Penal Record, should be made a week, if possible, before the prisoner's discharge, and should be in the form shown below, the estimated expense of the prison allowance of food supplied to the prisoner during the period of sentence, and the rate at which calculated, being given in the second column, and any remarks the Governor thinks it desirable to make, in the column provided for that purpose (1,651).

By order,

S. H. Douglas, Secretary.

——Prison.

Report of Committal of a Vagrant or offender against the laws in force for the relief of the destitute poor, who has 4s. or upwards in possession (under Circular 446):—

Amount of Cash in Prisoner's possession on committal.	Estimated expense of Prisoner's allowance of food during sentence, and rate per day at which calculated for each class of diet supplied.	Remarks of Governor.	Decision of Board.

Circular No. 447.

General Prisons Board, Dublin Castle,
4th March, 1896.

To the Governors (or other Officers in charge) of H. M. Prisons.

I am directed by the General Prisons Board to call your attention to No. XXV. of the Regulations as to fuel and light allowances, issued with Circular 272, in which it is pointed out that the scale fixes the maximum issues allowed, but that the *full quantities should not be issued or drawn by an officer for any quarters if not actually required for consumption in such quarters.*

In doing so, I am to state that the Board consider that in prisons where there is a mess or sitting room available, fires should not be lighted in the sleeping rooms, save under exceptional circumstances, with the special sanction of the Governor (2,170).

By order,
S. H. Douglas, Secretary.

APPENDIX

TO

EIGHTEENTH REPORT OF THE GENERAL PRISONS BOARD.

PART II.

LOCAL PRISON TABLES.

TABLE I.—RETURN of COMMITMENTS to the several LOCAL

PRISONS.	CONVICTED.						
	CRIMINAL PROCEEDINGS.						
	Drunkenness.	Under Larceny Acts.	Under Vagrant Acts.	Under Poor Law Acts.	Under Revenue Laws.	By Naval or Military Courts.	[illegible]
TOTAL, M. & F.,	12,[illegible]	1,904	1,049	218	90	214	10,[illegible]
MALES.							
Larger Prisons.							
Armagh,	453	60	28	2	4	–	[illegible]
Belfast,	1,548	318	84	44	8	9	1,1[illegible]
Castlebar,	97	13	8	6	21	–	[illegible]
Clonmel,	309	44	14	7	–	12	[illegible]
Cork, Male,	738	56	81	20	–	69	737
Dundalk,	191	46	22	9	1	8	[illegible]
Galway,	181	55	34	6	15	6	244
Kilkenny,	204	66	75	–	–	17	244
Kilmainham,	587	345	77	6	1	8	970
Limerick, Male,	495	48	51	16	–	14	469
Londonderry,	228	42	13	8	5	7	381
Mountjoy,	1,102	229	106	–	–	29	1,713
Sligo,	218	24	7	3	5	1	194
Tralee,	161	17	4	9	–	8	188
Tullamore,	256	61	25	7	–	17	249
Waterford,	457	85	18	5	10	–	169
Wexford,	161	20	10	7	7	5	51
Minor Prisons.							
Carrick-on-Shannon,	97	–	–	9	–	–	9
Drogheda,	116	–	10	4	2	–	28
Enniskillen,	74	8	3	–	1	–	19
Mullingar,	119	5	–	–	–	–	68
Omagh,	184	–	8	–	–	5	10
Wicklow,	34	4	8	–	–	11	36
Total Males,	6,078	1,485	632	168	78	214	7,516
FEMALES.							
Larger Prisons.							
Armagh,	173	17	34	–	1	–	89
Belfast,	1,239	166	25	4	–	–	399
Castlebar,	50	9	5	–	7	–	93
Cork, Female,	221	26	74	4	–	–	257
Galway,	57	19	7	8	2	–	98
Grangegorman,	1,804	182	110	–	–	–	1,[illegible]
Limerick, Female,	298	96	23	10	–	–	219
Londonderry,	124	16	62	3	–	–	115
Sligo,	63	9	16	1	1	–	24
Tralee,	23	11	3	1	–	–	38
Tullamore,	68	14	11	8	–	–	57
Waterford,	185	14	10	6	1	–	139
Wexford,	23	6	7	4	–	–	19
Minor Prisons.							
Carrick-on-Shannon,	20	–	–	–	–	–	8
Drogheda,	40	–	4	8	–	–	1
Enniskillen,	27	1	2	8	–	–	5
Mullingar,	61	8	1	–	–	–	12
Omagh,	23	1	6	–	–	–	5
Wicklow,	7	8	–	–	–	–	1
Total Females,	5,250	469	417	50	12	–	3,[illegible]

NOTE.—In the above Return, some of the "convicted" prisoners also appear as "not convicted" opposite other [illegible]

Prisons from 1st January, 1895, to 31st December, 1895.

1st Class Misdemeanants.				Not Convicted.				
Contempt of Court.	Others.	Debtors.	Total.	Acquitted on Trial, Remanded, and Discharged, or otherwise disposed of.	Remaining Untried.	Total.	Total Commitments.	Prisons.
67	-	86	27,217	3,105	175	3,307	31,224	TOTAL M. & F.
				MALES.				
								Larger Prisons.
-	-	8	721	71	6	77	798	Armagh.
-	-	4	3,108	417	18	435	[illegible]	Belfast.
4	-	-	349	53	5	58	407	Castlebar.
8	-	9	683	71	7	78	759	Clonmel.
6	-	1	1,082	160	16	176	[illegible]	Cork, Male.
1	-	4	510	55	1	50	[illegible]	Dundalk.
5	-	1	480	57	4	61	547	Galway.
3	-	8	711	103	5	108	819	Kilkenny.
6	-	17	[illegible]	710	[illegible]	751	3,775	Kilmainham.
4	-	6	1,059	178	[illegible]	201	[illegible]	Limerick, Male.
8	-	5	604	56	6	62	670	Londonderry.
-	-	16	[illegible]	-	-	-	[illegible]	Mountjoy.
8	-	-	441	53	7	60	501	Sligo.
-	-	5	344	58	8	64	[illegible]	Tralee.
1	-	8	508	47	8	55	548	Tullamore.
8	-	2	630	58	4	62	[illegible]	Waterford.
6	-	2	370	38	4	48	418	Wexford.
								Minor Prisons.
-	-	-	49	54	6	60	104	Carrick-on-Shannon.
-	-	-	156	54	1	55	211	Drogheda.
-	-	-	93	49	-	49	142	Enniskillen.
-	-	1	153	88	-	88	241	Mullingar.
-	-	7	159	50	2	52	211	Omagh.
-	-	-	80	68	1	69	149	Wicklow.
56	-	78	18,324	2,575	144	2,719	21,043	Total Males.
				FEMALES.				
								Larger Prisons.
-	-	-	313	14	-	14	327	Armagh.
1	-	-	3,212	100	3	103	3,316	Belfast.
-	-	-	102	17	-	17	119	Castlebar.
-	-	1	990	40	3	43	1,034	Cork, Female.
1	-	-	181	7	-	7	189	Galway.
4	-	-	3,878	160	21	201	[illegible]	Grangegorman.
-	-	-	628	88	6	92	720	Limerick, Female.
-	-	1	423	7	1	8	430	Londonderry.
3	-	-	153	11	1	12	166	Sligo.
-	-	-	60	8	-	8	68	Tralee.
1	-	-	307	6	4	10	317	Tullamore.
-	-	-	561	10	8	18	573	Waterford.
1	-	-	65	8	-	8	69	Wexford.
								Minor Prisons.
-	-	-	23	7	-	7	30	Carrick-on-Shannon.
-	-	-	53	22	-	22	75	Drogheda.
-	-	-	35	14	-	14	49	Enniskillen.
-	-	-	82	19	-	19	101	Mullingar.
-	-	1	46	10	-	10	56	Omagh.
-	-	-	10	4	-	4	14	Wicklow.
11	-	8	8,893	530	31	588	10,181	Total Females.

prisons to which they had previously been committed on the same charge. The total net number of was [illegible]

TABLE II.—NUMBER of PRISONERS in each PRISON on the First Day of each Month during the Year ended 31st December, 1895 (at Unlock).

PRISONS.	1st Jan.	1st Feb.	1st March.	1st April.	1st May.	1st June.	1st July.	1st Aug.	1st Sept.	1st Oct.	1st Nov.	1st Dec.
TOTAL, M. & F.,	[illegible]	[illegible]	1,71[illegible]	1,74[illegible]	2,016	2,16[illegible]	2,174	[illegible]	[illegible]	[illegible]	[illegible]	2,316?
MALES.												
Larger Prisons.												
Armagh,	84	67	70	70	[illegible]	[illegible]	84	47	[illegible]	48	62	81
Belfast,	[illegible]	[illegible]	[illegible]	[illegible]	674?	[illegible]	[illegible]	[illegible]	[illegible]	611?	[illegible]	[illegible]
Castlebar,	[illegible]	42	43	[illegible]	35?	40	[illegible]	[illegible]	16	16	[illegible]	[illegible]
Clonmel,	67?	[illegible]	46	46	[illegible]	45?	61	81	[illegible]	74	61	[illegible]
Cork Male,	[illegible]	[illegible]	134?	[illegible]	179?	175	[illegible]	[illegible]	[illegible]	277?	157?	219?
Dundalk,	[illegible]	57?	[illegible]	[illegible]	64	[illegible]	[illegible]	[illegible]	[illegible]	[illegible]	[illegible]	[illegible]
Galway,	51	61	[illegible]	[illegible]	41	[illegible]	[illegible]	[illegible]	[illegible]	[illegible]	[illegible]	[illegible]
Kilkenny,	[illegible]	[illegible]	[illegible]	[illegible]	[illegible]	91	[illegible]	[illegible]	[illegible]	[illegible]	[illegible]	[illegible]
Kilmainham,	[illegible]	[illegible]	[illegible]	[illegible]	[illegible]	[illegible]	[illegible]	[illegible]	[illegible]	[illegible]	146?	[illegible]
Limerick Male,	[illegible]	[illegible]	[illegible]	[illegible]	[illegible]	[illegible]	[illegible]	[illegible]	[illegible]	[illegible]	[illegible]	[illegible]
Londonderry,	[illegible]	44?	[illegible]	[illegible]	67?	[illegible]	[illegible]	[illegible]	71?	[illegible]	71?	[illegible]
Mountjoy,	[illegible]	[illegible]	[illegible]	[illegible]	[illegible]	[illegible]	[illegible]	[illegible]	[illegible]	[illegible]	[illegible]	[illegible]
Sligo,	[illegible]	[illegible]	[illegible]	[illegible]	51?	[illegible]	[illegible]	[illegible]	[illegible]	[illegible]	[illegible]	[illegible]
Tralee,	[illegible]	[illegible]	[illegible]	[illegible]	77	[illegible]	[illegible]	[illegible]	[illegible]	[illegible]	[illegible]	[illegible]
Tullamore,	[illegible]	75?	[illegible]	[illegible]	76	[illegible]	[illegible]	[illegible]	[illegible]	[illegible]	[illegible]	71?
Waterford,	[illegible]	[illegible]	[illegible]	[illegible]	[illegible]	[illegible]	[illegible]	71	[illegible]	[illegible]	[illegible]	[illegible]
Wexford,	[illegible]	[illegible]	17	17	15	[illegible]	[illegible]	81?	[illegible]	27?	[illegible]	34?
Minor Prisons.												
Carrick-on-Shannon	[illegible]	–	[illegible]	1	[illegible]	[illegible]	[illegible]	–	[illegible]	1	[illegible]	[illegible]
Drogheda,	[illegible]	–	–	[illegible]	5	1	[illegible]	[illegible]	[illegible]	[illegible]	[illegible]	[illegible]
Enniskillen,	[illegible]	[illegible]	1	[illegible]	–	–	[illegible]	1	[illegible]	–	1	[illegible]
Mullingar,	[illegible]	[illegible]	[illegible]	[illegible]	7	[illegible]	[illegible]	[illegible]	[illegible]	[illegible]	[illegible]	[illegible]
Omagh,	[illegible]	4	[illegible]	[illegible]	[illegible]	[illegible]	11	[illegible]	1	[illegible]	[illegible]	[illegible]
Wicklow,	[illegible]	1	[illegible]	1	[illegible]	[illegible]	[illegible]	[illegible]	1	[illegible]	–	[illegible]
Total Males,	1,51[illegible]	[illegible],57[illegible]	1,[illegible]	1,[illegible]	1,61[illegible]	1,54[illegible]	1,[illegible]	1,7[illegible]	1,7[illegible]	1,[illegible]	1,7[illegible]	1,797?
FEMALES.												
Larger Prisons.												
Armagh,	[illegible]	17	[illegible]	[illegible]	[illegible]	31?	[illegible]	[illegible]	41	[illegible]	[illegible]	[illegible]
Belfast,	[illegible]	156?	[illegible]	[illegible]	[illegible]	[illegible]	[illegible]	[illegible]	[illegible]	127?	[illegible]	[illegible]
Castlebar,	4	7	[illegible]	7	7	12?	[illegible]	10	5	6	[illegible]	[illegible]
Cork Female,	[illegible]	[illegible]	[illegible]	[illegible]	[illegible]	87?	97?	[illegible]	116?	97	[illegible]	[illegible]
Galway,	[illegible]	16	[illegible]	[illegible]	[illegible]	14	13?	[illegible]	[illegible]	16	[illegible]	[illegible]
Grangegorman,	[illegible]	[illegible]	[illegible]	[illegible]	[illegible]	[illegible]	179?	[illegible]	[illegible]	274?	[illegible]	[illegible]
Limerick Female	[illegible]	[illegible]	[illegible]	[illegible]	[illegible]	[illegible]	[illegible]	[illegible]	[illegible]	[illegible]	[illegible]	[illegible]
Londonderry,	[illegible]	[illegible]	[illegible]	27?	[illegible]	[illegible]	[illegible]	[illegible]	[illegible]	[illegible]	[illegible]	[illegible]
Sligo,	11	[illegible]	19?	[illegible]	19?	[illegible]	[illegible]	[illegible]	[illegible]	17	17	17?
Tralee,	[illegible]	[illegible]	[illegible]	[illegible]	[illegible]	4	[illegible]	[illegible]	4?	[illegible]	[illegible]	[illegible]
Tullamore,	[illegible]	[illegible]	16?	6	16?	21	[illegible]	[illegible]	[illegible]	17	[illegible]	[illegible]
Waterford,	[illegible]	[illegible]	15?	14?	[illegible]	[illegible]	[illegible]	[illegible]	[illegible]	[illegible]	[illegible]	[illegible]
Wexford,	4	[illegible]	1	[illegible]	6	1	[illegible]	[illegible]	[illegible]	[illegible]	[illegible]	4
Minor Prisons.												
Carrick-on-Shannon	1	–	–	–	1	–	[illegible]	–	[illegible]	1	–	–
Drogheda,	–	–	1	[illegible]	[illegible]	[illegible]	[illegible]	[illegible]	–	1	1	–
Enniskillen,	–	1	–	–	–	–	–	1	[illegible]	1	[illegible]	[illegible]
Mullingar,	1	–	[illegible]	[illegible]	[illegible]	1	1	[illegible]	–	1	[illegible]	[illegible]
Omagh,	–	–	–	1	–	–	1	–	1	1	[illegible]	–
Wicklow,	–	–	–	–	–	1	1	–	–	–	1	4
Total Females,	511	467?	383?	483?	[illegible]	[illegible]	579	[illegible]	650?	[illegible]	631?	[illegible]

Table III.—Daily Average Number of Prisoners in Custody, &c., &c., from 1st January, 1895, to 31st December, 1895.

Name of Prisons.	Daily Average Number of Prisoners, including those under Civil Process.			Highest Number confined at any one time (both Sexes).		Lowest Number confined at any one time (both Sexes).		Highest Number of Male Prisoners confined at any one time.		Highest Number of Female Prisoners confined at any one time.		Lowest Number of Male Prisoners confined at any one time.		Lowest Number of Female Prisoners confined at any one time.	
	M.	F.	Total.	No.	Date.	No.	Date.	No.	Date.	No.	Date.	No.	Date.	No.	Date.
Larger Prisons.															
Armagh,	46·5	[illegible]	[illegible]	[illegible]	[illegible]	[illegible]	[illegible]	[illegible]	[illegible]	[illegible]	[illegible]	[illegible]	[illegible]	16	[illegible]
Belfast,	[illegible]	110·16	[illegible]	[illegible]	[illegible]	[illegible]	[illegible]	[illegible]	[illegible]	141	[illegible]	[illegible]	[illegible]	[illegible]	[illegible]
Castlebar,	[illegible]	[illegible]	[illegible]	[illegible]	[illegible]	[illegible]	[illegible]	[illegible]	[illegible]	[illegible]	[illegible]	[illegible]	[illegible]	[illegible]	[illegible]
Clonmel,	[illegible]	–	[illegible]	[illegible]	[illegible]	[illegible]	[illegible]	[illegible]	[illegible]	–	–	[illegible]	[illegible]	–	–
Cork, Male,	[illegible]	–	[illegible]	[illegible]	[illegible]	[illegible]	[illegible]	[illegible]	[illegible]	–	–	[illegible]	[illegible]	–	–
Cork, Female,	–	84·	84·	116	1·9	[illegible]	[illegible]	–	–	116	1·9	–	–	[illegible]	[illegible]
Dundalk,	[illegible]	–	[illegible]	[illegible]	[illegible]	[illegible]	[illegible]	[illegible]	[illegible]	–	–	[illegible]	[illegible]	–	–
Galway,	[illegible]	[illegible]	[illegible]	[illegible]	[illegible]	[illegible]	[illegible]	[illegible]	[illegible]	[illegible]	[illegible]	[illegible]	[illegible]	7	[illegible]
Grangegorman,	–	[illegible]	[illegible]	[illegible]	[illegible]	[illegible]	[illegible]	–	–	[illegible]	[illegible]	–	–	[illegible]	[illegible]
Kilkenny,	[illegible]	–	[illegible]	[illegible]	[illegible]	[illegible]	[illegible]	[illegible]	[illegible]	–	–	[illegible]	[illegible]	–	–
Kilmainham,	[illegible]	–	[illegible]	[illegible]	[illegible]	[illegible]	[illegible]	[illegible]	[illegible]	–	–	[illegible]	[illegible]	–	–
Limerick, Male,	[illegible]	–	[illegible]	[illegible]	[illegible]	[illegible]	[illegible]	[illegible]	[illegible]	–	–	[illegible]	[illegible]	–	–
Limerick, Female,	–	[illegible]	[illegible]	[illegible]	[illegible]	[illegible]	[illegible]	–	–	[illegible]	[illegible]	–	–	[illegible]	[illegible]
Londonderry,	[illegible]	[illegible]	[illegible]	[illegible]	[illegible]	[illegible]	[illegible]	[illegible]	[illegible]	[illegible]	[illegible]	[illegible]	[illegible]	[illegible]	[illegible]
Mountjoy,	[illegible]	–	[illegible]	[illegible]	[illegible]	[illegible]	[illegible]	[illegible]	[illegible]	–	–	[illegible]	[illegible]	–	–
Sligo,	[illegible]	[illegible]	[illegible]	[illegible]	[illegible]	[illegible]	[illegible]	[illegible]	[illegible]	[illegible]	[illegible]	[illegible]	[illegible]	[illegible]	[illegible]
Tralee,	[illegible]	[illegible]	[illegible]	[illegible]	[illegible]	[illegible]	[illegible]	[illegible]	[illegible]	[illegible]	[illegible]	[illegible]	[illegible]	[illegible]	[illegible]
Tullamore,	[illegible]	[illegible]	[illegible]	[illegible]	[illegible]	[illegible]	[illegible]	[illegible]	[illegible]	[illegible]	[illegible]	[illegible]	[illegible]	[illegible]	[illegible]
Waterford,	[illegible]	[illegible]	[illegible]	[illegible]	[illegible]	[illegible]	[illegible]	[illegible]	[illegible]	[illegible]	[illegible]	[illegible]	[illegible]	[illegible]	[illegible]
Wexford,	[illegible]	[illegible]	[illegible]	[illegible]	[illegible]	[illegible]	[illegible]	[illegible]	[illegible]	[illegible]	[illegible]	[illegible]	[illegible]	[illegible]	[illegible]
Minor Prisons.															
Carrick-on-Shannon,	[illegible]	[illegible]	[illegible]	14	[illegible]	–	[illegible]	[illegible]	[illegible]	[illegible]	[illegible]	–	[illegible]	–	[illegible]
[illegible]	[illegible]	[illegible]	[illegible]	[illegible]	[illegible]	–	[illegible]	[illegible]	[illegible]	[illegible]	[illegible]	–	[illegible]	–	[illegible]
[illegible]	[illegible]	[illegible]	[illegible]	[illegible]	[illegible]	–	[illegible]	[illegible]	[illegible]	[illegible]	[illegible]	–	[illegible]	–	[illegible]

TABLE IV.—SENTENCES, PREVIOUS CONVICTIONS, AGES, BIRTHPLACE, RELIGIOUS PROFESSIONS, and OCCUPATION of CONVICTED CRIMINALS received into PRISON during the year 1895.

1. NATURE OF SENTENCES.

	M.	F.	Total.
Death,	1	1	2
Penal Servitude,	[illegible]	13	168
Forfeiture of Licence (where this is the only Punishment),	6	-	6
Imprisonment—			
Imprisonment without option of Fine—			
With Hard Labour,	4,651	1,271	[illegible]
Without Hard Labour,	1,324	677	
Imprisonment in default of Payment of Fine—			
With Hard Labour,	3,576	1,169	17,718
Without Hard Labour,	7,145	[illegible]	
Imprisonment in default of Bail,	170	[illegible]	[illegible]

	M.	F.	Total.
Imprisonment—			
First class Misdemeanants,	-	1	1
Prisoners convicted by Courts Martial,	[illegible]	-	[illegible]
Total,	[illegible]	[illegible]	[illegible]
Cases in which a Second Punishment accompanies Penal Servitude or Imprisonment—			
Flogging,	-	-	-
Whipping,	-	-	4
Sentence of Police Supervision,	-	-	[illegible]
Forfeiture or Revocation of Licence,	-	-	13

2. PREVIOUS CONVICTIONS.

(Exclusive of Prisoners convicted by Courts-Martial.)

Number of Prisoners who had been previously Convicted—	M.	F.	Total.
Once,	[illegible]	[illegible]	3,114
Twice,	1,[illegible]	[illegible]	1,[illegible]
Thrice,	[illegible]	[illegible]	1,[illegible]
Four times,	712	[illegible]	1,[illegible]
Five times,	[illegible]	[illegible]	[illegible]
Six to ten times,	1,[illegible]	[illegible]	[illegible]
Eleven to twenty times,	1,[illegible]	1,[illegible]	[illegible]
Above twenty times,	1,[illegible]	[illegible]	[illegible]
Total,	10,731	[illegible]	17,[illegible]

Number of Prisoners who had undergone previous Sentences of Penal Servitude—	M.	F.	Total.
Once,	[illegible]	[illegible]	170
Two,	[illegible]	[illegible]	[illegible]
Three,	8	3	11
Four,	1	-	1
Five or more,	1	6	7
Total,	[illegible]	[illegible]	[illegible]

3. AGE AND BIRTHPLACE.

(Exclusive of Prisoners convicted by Courts-Martial.)

Age and Sex—	M.	F.	Total.
Under 12 years,	[illegible]	-	[illegible]
12 years and under 16,	[illegible]	[illegible]	[illegible]
16 and under 21,	[illegible]	[illegible]	[illegible]
21 and under 30,	[illegible]	[illegible]	[illegible]
30 and under 40,	[illegible]	[illegible]	7,1[illegible]
40 and under 50,	[illegible]	[illegible]	[illegible]
50 and under 60,	1,[illegible]	[illegible]	[illegible]
60 and above,	1,[illegible]	[illegible]	1,[illegible]
Age not ascertained,	1	-	1
Total,	[illegible]	[illegible]	[illegible]

Birthplace—	M.	F.	Total.
England,	[illegible]	[illegible]	[illegible]
Wales,	[illegible]	[illegible]	[illegible]
Scotland,	[illegible]	[illegible]	[illegible]
Ireland,	14,[illegible]	[illegible]	[illegible]
Colonies and India,	[illegible]	[illegible]	[illegible]
Foreign Countries,	[illegible]	[illegible]	[illegible]
Not ascertained,	-	1	1
Total,	[illegible]	[illegible]	[illegible]

4. RELIGIOUS PROFESSIONS AND PREVIOUS OCCUPATIONS.

(Exclusive of Prisoners convicted by Courts-Martial.)

	M.	F.	Total.
Religious Professions—			
Protestant Episcopalians of Ireland,	1,7[illegible]	1,[illegible]	[illegible]
Presbyterians,	[illegible]	[illegible]	1,[illegible]
Roman Catholics,	14,1[illegible]	7,[illegible]	[illegible]
Other Religious Professions,	41	2	43
None, or not ascertained,	11	[illegible]	[illegible]
Total,	[illegible]	[illegible]	[illegible]
Previous Occupations—			
Domestic Servants,	[illegible]	[illegible]	1,[illegible]
Labourers, Charwomen, Needlewomen,	10,[illegible]	[illegible]	11,[illegible]
Factory Workers,	[illegible]	[illegible]	[illegible]

Previous Occupations—*con.*	M.	F.	Total.
Mechanics and Skilled Workers,	[illegible]	[illegible]	[illegible]
Foremen and Overlookers of Labour,	[illegible]	[illegible]	[illegible]
Shopmen, Shopwomen, Clerks,	[illegible]	[illegible]	[illegible]
Shopkeepers and Dealers,	[illegible]	1,1[illegible]	[illegible]
Professional Employments,	[illegible]	-	[illegible]
Sailors, Marines, Soldiers,	[illegible]	-	[illegible]
Prostitutes,	-	[illegible]	[illegible]
No occupation,	[illegible]	[illegible]	[illegible]
Occupation not ascertained,	[illegible]	[illegible]	[illegible]
Total,	[illegible]	[illegible]	[illegible]

TABLE V.

SENTENCES ON CONVICTED PRISONERS, &c.

TABLE V.—SENTENCES ON CONVICTED PRISONERS (exclusive of those
during the year ending

(Cumulative sentences are returned as equal to their united length. Concurrent sentences

Prisons.	Death (executed).	Penal Servitude for: Life.	Penal Servitude for: Other terms.	Imprisonment for: 2 Years and above 1.	1 Year and above [illegible] Months.	[illegible] Months and above [illegible] Months.	[illegible] Months and above 11 Months.	[illegible] Months and above 10 Months.	[illegible] Months and above 9 Months.	[illegible] Months and above 8 Months.	[illegible] Months and above 7 Months.	7 Months and above 6 Months.	6 Months and above 5 Months.	5 Months and above 4 Months.	4 Months and above 3 Months.	3 Months and above 11 Weeks.	11 Weeks and above 10 Weeks.	[illegible] Weeks and above [illegible] Weeks.	[illegible] Weeks and above [illegible] Weeks.	[illegible] Weeks and above [illegible] Weeks.
Larger Prisons.																				
Armagh,	–	–	5	–	1	3	6	–	–	1	1	–	13	5	3	[illegible]	9	5	[illegible]	15
Belfast,	–	–	7	–	1	9	[illegible]	–	–	[illegible]	6	1	101	61	[illegible]	[illegible]	–	8	–	[illegible]
Castlebar,	–	1	–	–	–	1	–	–	1	–	1	5	2	4	[illegible]	7	–	1	17	7
Clonmel,	–	–	8	–	6	1	5	1	–	3	1	1	7	–	5	[illegible]	–	[illegible]	8	15
Cork, Male,	–	1	[illegible]	–	–	1	16	–	1	4	9	5	27	6	[illegible]	[illegible]	[illegible]	6	[illegible]	6
Cork, Female,	–	–	1	–	1	1	4	–	–	–	–	–	[illegible]	4	[illegible]	1	–	1	[illegible]	–
Dundalk,	–	–	3	–	–	–	5	–	1	–	–	1	4	–	5	[illegible]	6	–	[illegible]	6
Galway,	–	–	8	–	–	4	3	–	1	1	–	4	[illegible]	11	9	[illegible]	7	3	[illegible]	[illegible]
Grangegorman, Female,	–	–	7	–	–	–	9	–	–	1	–	–	67	–	[illegible]	[illegible]	[illegible]	–	–	[illegible]
Kilkenny,	–	–	4	–	–	6	6	–	–	5	–	–	19	1	11	[illegible]	–	3	[illegible]	7
Kilmainham,	–	–	3	–	1	16	5	3	6	5	1	16	10	19	[illegible]	[illegible]	1	[illegible]	[illegible]	[illegible]
Limerick, Male,	–	–	4	–	–	5	5	–	–	1	1	1	15	3	9	[illegible]	6	7	[illegible]	[illegible]
Limerick, Female,	1	–	–	–	–	–	–	–	–	–	–	–	7	1	4	[illegible]	[illegible]	6	[illegible]	[illegible]
Londonderry,	–	–	3	–	–	8	4	1	–	5	1	3	12	–	11	[illegible]	–	4	1	[illegible]
Mountjoy,	–	–	[illegible]	–	9	6	[illegible]	–	–	4	1	1	87	5	[illegible]	87	3	4	[illegible]	4
Sligo,	–	–	5	–	–	–	1	–	–	3	1	–	21	–	6	[illegible]	–	1	[illegible]	9
Tralee,	–	–	–	–	1	8	–	–	1	–	–	[illegible]	9	–	[illegible]	–	–	1	[illegible]	1
Tullamore,	–	–	5	–	9	1	3	–	–	5	1	–	[illegible]	1	13	[illegible]	[illegible]	9	[illegible]	7
Waterford,	–	–	3	–	–	–	–	–	–	1	–	3	6	8	17	[illegible]	–	3	7	[illegible]
Wexford,	–		–	–	–	–	3	1	–	–	8	1	5	–	8	[illegible]	1	–	[illegible]	–
Minor Prisons.																				
Carrick-on-Shannon,	–	–	–	–	–	–	–	–	–	–	–	–	–	–	–	–	–	–	–	–
Drogheda,	–	–	–	–	–	–	–	–	–	–	–	–	–	–	–	–	–	–	–	–
Enniskillen,	–	–	–	–	–	–	–	–	–	–	–	–	–	–	–	–	–	–	–	–
Mullingar,	–	–	–	–	–	–	–	–	–	–	–	–	–	–	–	–	–	–	–	–
Omagh,	–	–	–	–	–	–	–	–	–	–	–	–	–	–	–	–	–	–	–	–
Wicklow,	–	–	–	–	–	–	–	–	–	–	–	–	–	–	–	–	–	–	–	–
Total,	1	7	[illegible]	–	11	[illegible]	[illegible]	6	[illegible]	[illegible]	[illegible]	[illegible]	[illegible]	75	[illegible]	[illegible]	[illegible]	[illegible]	[illegible]	[illegible]

convicted by Courts-Martial) committed to the under-mentioned
31st December, 1895.

are returned as equal to one of them, or to the longer when they are of unequal l

Imprisonment for														
7 Weeks and above 6 Weeks.	6 Weeks and above 5 Weeks.	5 Weeks and above 4 Weeks.	4 Weeks and above 3 Weeks.	3 Weeks and above 2 Weeks.	2 Weeks and above 1 Week.	1 Week.	6 Days.	5 Days.	4 Days.	3 Days.	2 Days.	1 Day.	Total Sentences of Imprisonment.	Total Sentenced.

[illegible]

[illegible]	[illegible]	[illegible]	[illegible]	[illegible]	[illegible]	[illegible]	[illegible]	[illegible]
[illegible]	[illegible]	[illegible]	[illegible]	[illegible]	[illegible]	[illegible]	[illegible]	[illegible]
[illegible]	[illegible]	[illegible]	[illegible]	[illegible]	[illegible]	[illegible]	[illegible]	[illegible]
[illegible]	[illegible]	[illegible]	[illegible]	[illegible]	[illegible]	[illegible]	[illegible]	[illegible]
[illegible]	[illegible]	[illegible]	[illegible]	[illegible]	[illegible]	[illegible]	[illegible]	[illegible]
[illegible]	[illegible]	[illegible]	[illegible]	[illegible]	[illegible]	[illegible]	[illegible]	[illegible]
[illegible]	[illegible]	[illegible]	[illegible]	[illegible]	-	[illegible]	.	.

[illegible]

[illegible]	[illegible]	[illegible]	[illegible]	[illegible]	[illegible]	[illegible]	[illegible]	[illegible]
[illegible]	[illegible]	[illegible]	[illegible]	[illegible]	[illegible]	[illegible]	[illegible]	[illegible]
[illegible]	[illegible]	[illegible]	[illegible]	[illegible]	[illegible]	[illegible]	[illegible]	[illegible]
[illegible]	[illegible]	[illegible]	[illegible]	[illegible]	[illegible]	[illegible]	[illegible]	[illegible]
[illegible]	[illegible]	[illegible]	[illegible]	[illegible]	[illegible]	[illegible]	-	-
[illegible]	[illegible]	[illegible]	[illegible]	[illegible]	-	[illegible]	-	.

[illegible]

TABLE VII.—Cases of Sickness amongst Prisoners, in the undermentioned Local Prisons during the year ended 31st December, 1895.

Prison.	Number in Prison Hospital.		Daily average Number in Hospital.		Number of Cases of Illness or Disease prescribed for out of Hospital.	
	M.	F.	M.	F.	M.	F.
Armagh,	-	2	-	·080	303	159
Belfast,	16	4	·33	·10	1,046	391
Castlebar,	1	-	·008	-	128	40
Clonmel,	17	-	·74	-	304	-
Cork, Male,	104	-	2·045	-	1,843	-
Cork, Female,	-	69	-	3·	-	1,450
Dundalk,	3	-	·21	-	122	-
Galway,	37	4	1·246	·269	191	307
Grangegorman,	-	179	-	4·	-	2,050
Kilkenny,	7	-	·19	-	430	-
Kilmainham,	31	-	1·63	-	391	-
Limerick, Male,	19	-	·34	-	604	-
Limerick, Female,	-	2	-	·03	-	260
Londonderry,	38	17	2·12	·03	390	225
Mountjoy,	639	-	6·109	-	6,032	-
Sligo,	7	4	·16	·16	216	167
Tralee,	4	1	·91	·008	191	81
Tullamore,	9	3	·25	·06	325	78
Waterford,	5	8	·18	·07	310	181
Wexford,	-	-	-	-	210	17
Total Males,	[illegible]	-	15·812	-	19,815	-
Total Females,	-	296	-	9·410	-	5,417
Total M. and F.,	1,146		[illegible]		[illegible]	

TABLE VIII.

DISEASES FOR WHICH PRISONERS HAVE BEEN TREATED, &c.

[illegible]	[illegible]
[illegible]	[illegible]
[illegible]	[illegible]
[illegible]	[illegible]
[illegible]	[illegible]
[illegible]	[illegible]
[illegible]	[illegible]
[illegible]	[illegible]
[illegible]	[illegible]
[illegible]	[illegible]

[illegible]	[illegible]	[illegible]	[illegible]	[illegible]	[illegible]	[illegible]	[illegible]	[illegible]	[illegible]	[illegible]	[illegible]
[illegible]	[illegible]	[illegible]	[illegible]	[illegible]	[illegible]	[illegible]	[illegible]	[illegible]	[illegible]	[illegible]	[illegible]

[illegible]

[illegible]

[illegible]	[illegible]	[illegible]	[illegible]	[illegible]	[illegible]	[illegible]	[illegible]	[illegible]	[illegible]
[illegible]	[illegible]	[illegible]	[illegible]	[illegible]	[illegible]	[illegible]	[illegible]	[illegible]	[illegible]
[illegible]	[illegible]	[illegible]	[illegible]	[illegible]	[illegible]	[illegible]	[illegible]	[illegible]	[illegible]
[illegible]	[illegible]	[illegible]	[illegible]	[illegible]	[illegible]	[illegible]	[illegible]	[illegible]	[illegible]
[illegible]	[illegible]	[illegible]	[illegible]	[illegible]	[illegible]	[illegible]	[illegible]	[illegible]	[illegible]

TABLE X.—Deaths in Local Prisons and their Causes during the year ended 31st December, 18[illegible].

(A.)—Deaths exclusive of Executions.

Prison in which Death occurred.	No.	Sex.	Initials of Name.	Age.	Date of Committal.	Date of Conviction.	Sentence.	Date of Death.	Disease, &c., which caused death.	Whether Disease [illegible]	General Health on reception into Local Prison.	Number of previous Convictions.	Previous Occupation.
[illegible]	[illegible]	[illegible]	[illegible]	[illegible]	[illegible]	[illegible]	[illegible]	[illegible]	[illegible]	[illegible]	Good	[illegible]	[illegible]
[illegible]	[illegible]	[illegible]	[illegible]	[illegible]	[illegible]	[illegible]	[illegible]	[illegible]	[illegible]	[illegible]	[illegible]	[illegible]	[illegible]
[illegible]	[illegible]	[illegible]	[illegible]	[illegible]	[illegible]	[illegible]	[illegible]	[illegible]	[illegible]	[illegible]	Bad	[illegible]	[illegible]

(B.)—Executions.

Prison in which Death occurred.	No.	Sex.	Initials of Name.	Age.	Date of Committal.	Date of Conviction.	Sentence.	Date of Death.	Disease, &c., which caused death.	Whether Disease [illegible]	General Health on reception into Local Prison.	Number of previous Convictions.	Previous Occupation.
[illegible]	1	[illegible]	[illegible]	[illegible]	[illegible]	[illegible]	[illegible]	[illegible]	[illegible]	—	Good	[illegible]	[illegible]

TABLE XI.—PARTICULARS of each case of INSANITY (amongst Prisoners)

(See paragraph 136 of Report

[illegible]	Education.	Occupation previous to Conviction.	Crime or Charge.	Date of Conviction (if Convicted).	Sentence (if sentenced).	Date of Reception into a Local Prison.	No

in Local Prisons, during Year ended 31st December, 1898

of Royal Commission, 1884).

No.	Mental Condition on Reception into a Local Prison.	Whether previously Insane.	Length of Imprisonment previous to first symptoms of Insanity (in cases originating in Prison).	Form of Insanity.	Termination of Case.			
					Recovered in Prison.	Removed to Asylum. Name of Asylum and Date of Removal.	Died in Prison with Date.	Remaining in Prison.
				ARMAGH.				
1	Insane,	Yes,	—	Delusional,	—	Armagh, 18. 12. 98,	—	
				BELFAST.				
2	Weak,	Not known,	—	Melancholia,	—	Belfast, [illegible]	—	
3	Insane,	Yes,	—	Religious mania,	—	do., 11. 8. 98,	—	
4	do.,	Not known,	—	Melancholia,	—	do., [illegible]	—	—
5	do.,	Yes,	—	Religious mania,	—	Dundrum, [illegible]	—	—
6	do.,	Not known,	—	Homicidal mania,	—	do., [illegible]	—	—
7	do.,	do.,	—	Idiotic,	—	do., [illegible]	—	—
8	do.,	Yes,	—	Religious mania,	—	Belfast, [illegible] 11. 98,	—	—
				CASTLEBAR.				
9	Insane,	Not known,	—	Mania,	—	Castlebar, 7. 4. 98,	—	—
10	do.,	do.,	—	do.,	—	do., 12. 8. 98,	—	—
11	do.,	do.,	—	do.,	—	do., [illegible] 98,	—	—
12	do.,	do.,	—	do.,	—	do., 15. 9. 98,	—	—
				CORK (Male).				
13	Good,	Not known,	40 days,	Melancholia,	—	Cork, [illegible] 98,	—	—
14	do.,	do.,	41 days,	Religious mania,	—	Dundrum, [illegible] 98,	—	—
15	Insane,	Yes,	—	Acute alcoholic mania,	—	Cork, 16. 7. 98,	—	—
16	Good,	No,	[illegible] days,	Sub-acute mania,	—	do., 16. 11. 98,	—	—
17	Fairly good,	Yes,	—	Homicidal mania,	—	Dundrum, 16. 12. 98,	—	—
18	Insane,	Not known,	—	Imbecile,	—	Cork, [illegible] 98,	—	—
				CORK (Female).				
19	Good,	No,	[illegible] days,	Melancholia,	—	Cork, 12. 8. 98,	—	—

TABLE XI.—PARTICULARS of each case of INSANITY (amongst Prisoners) in

Initials of Name.	Sex.	Age (Years).	Education.	Occupation previous to Conviction.	Crime or Charge.	Date of Conviction (if Convicted).	Sentence (if convicted).	Date of Reception into a Local Prison.	No.
					GALWAY.				
J. G.,	M.	[illegible]	R.W.	Fisherman,	Assault,	–	Remanded,	[illegible]	[illegible]
W. B.,	M.	[illegible]	W.	Pauper,	Disobedience of Workhouse Rules.	[illegible]	1 c. mth.,	[illegible]	[illegible]
					GRANGEGORMAN.				
E. G.,	F.	[illegible]	R.W.	Prostitute,	Trespass on Curragh,	[illegible]	I. 1 c. mth. or [illegible] II. 1 c. mth. or [illegible]	[illegible]	[illegible]
M. A. T.,	F.	[illegible]	do.	do.,	Drunk,	[illegible]	1 mth. or [illegible],	[illegible]	[illegible]
L. G. R.,	F.	[illegible]	do.	Servant,	Attempt suicide,	–	Remand,	[illegible]	[illegible]
E. G.,	F.	[illegible]	do.	Prostitute,	Assault and larceny,	–	Remanded,	[illegible]	[illegible]
M. A. M.,	F.	[illegible]	do.	—	Neglecting her children,	[illegible]	[illegible] c. mths.,	[illegible]	[illegible]
B. C.,	F.	[illegible]	do.	Charwoman,	Break glass,	[illegible]	[illegible] c. mths. or bail,	[illegible]	[illegible]
J. E.,	F.	[illegible]	do.	None,	False pretences,	–	To be kept in custody until the pleasure of the Lord Lieutenant be made known.	—	[illegible]
					KILMAINHAM.				
[illegible] C.,	M.	[illegible]	R.W.	Soldier and labourer,	Murder of his child,	–	To be detained during Lord Lieutenant's pleasure.	[illegible]	[illegible]
E. M.,	M.	76	R.	Widower,	Attempt suicide,	–	To be detained in custody until the pleasure of His Excellency the Lord Lieutenant be made known.	[illegible]	[illegible]
J. P.,	M.	[illegible]	R.W.	Blacksmith,	Illegal possession (2 cases).	[illegible]	I. 7 days, II. 7 days, and 14 days or bail.	[illegible]	[illegible]
D. H.,	M.	[illegible]	Supr.	Itinerant doctor,	Loitering with intent to commit felony,	–	—	[illegible]	[illegible]
J. F.,	M.	[illegible]	R.W.	Printer,	Assault occasioning grievous bodily harm,	–	To be detained in custody until the pleasure of His Excellency be made known.	[illegible]	[illegible]
J. M.,	M.	[illegible]	do.	Farmer,	Setting fire to a dwelling house,	[illegible]	To be kept in Kilmainham Prison until Her Majesty's pleasure be known.	[illegible]	[illegible]
A. R.,	M.	[illegible]	do.	Clerk,	Indecent exposure,	[illegible]	To be detained in Kilmainham Gaol until the pleasure of the Lord Lieutenant be known.	[illegible]	[illegible]
					LIMERICK (Male).				
J. D.,	M.	71	R.W.	Vagrant,	Vagrancy,	[illegible]	14 days h.l.,	[illegible]	[illegible]
M. F.,	M.	[illegible]	do.	Labourer,	Assault,	[illegible]	[illegible] c. mths. h.l.,	[illegible]	[illegible]
J. A.,	M.	[illegible]	do.	Farmer,	Riotous and violent behaviour in a churchyard during divine service.	12. 7. [illegible]	[illegible] c. mth.,	[illegible]	[illegible]
D. C.,	M.	[illegible]	do.	Tailor,	Breaking into a dwelling-house and stealing money, &c.	–	Remanded,	[illegible]	[illegible]
[illegible] O.,	M.	[illegible]	do.	Labourer,	I. Assault and hard [illegible] of [illegible]. II. Threatening language.	[illegible]	I. [illegible] c. mths. h.l. II. [illegible] c. mths., or bail,	[illegible]	[illegible]
J. M.,	M.	[illegible]	do.	Farmer,	Inflicting grievous bodily harm on J. M.	–	Remanded,	[illegible]	[illegible]

LOCAL PRISONS, during Year ended 31st December, 1895—continued.

No.	Mental Condition on Reception into a Local Prison.	Whether previously insane.	Length of Imprisonment previous to first symptoms of Insanity (in cases originating in Prison).	Form of Insanity.	Termination of Case. Recovered in Prison.	Removed to Asylum. Name of Asylum and Date of Removal.	Died in Prison with Date.	Remaining in Prison.
				GALWAY.				
[illegible]	Insane,	Not known,	—	Mania,	—	Ballinasloe, [illegible]	—	—
[illegible]	do.,	Doubtful,	—	Dementia,	—	do., [illegible]	—	—
				GRANGEGORMAN.				
[illegible]	Insane,	Yes,	—	Sub-acute mania,	—	Cork, [illegible]	—	—
[illegible]	do.,	do.,	—	Mania,	—	do., [illegible]	—	—
[illegible]	do.,	do.,	—	Acute mania,	—	Richmond, [illegible]	—	—
[illegible]	do.,	do.,	—	Sub-acute mania with delusions,	—	do., [illegible]	—	—
[illegible]	do.,	do.,	—	Dementia,	—	do., [illegible]	—	—
[illegible]	do.,	do.,	—	do.,	—	do., [illegible]	—	—
[illegible]	do.,	—	—	—	—	—	—	—
				KILMAINHAM.				
[illegible]	Insane,	Not known,	—	Melancholia,	—	Dundrum, [illegible]	—	—
[illegible]	do.,	do.,	—	do.,	—	Richmond, [illegible]	—	—
[illegible]	do.,	Probably,	—	Mania,	—	do., [illegible]	—	—
[illegible]	do.	Not known,	—	Delusional dementia,	—	do., [illegible]	—	—
[illegible]	do.,	do.,	—	Mania,	—	Dundrum, [illegible]	—	—
14	Not apparent,	Believed to be so.	—	Delusional dementia,	—	do., [illegible]	—	—
[illegible]	Doubtful,	Believed to be so.	—	Dementia,	—	—	—	Yes.
				LIMERICK (Male).				
[illegible]	Insane,	Not known,	—	Dementia,	—	Limerick, [illegible]	—	—
[illegible]	do.,	do.,	—	Mania, with homicidal tendencies	—	Dundrum, [illegible]	—	—
28	do.,	do.,	—	Melancholia with delusions.	—	Ennis, [illegible]	—	—
[illegible]	Fair,	do.,	[illegible] days.	Acute mania with delusions.	—	Limerick, [illegible]	—	—
[illegible]	Insane,	Yes,	—	Recurrent mania with suicidal tendencies.	—	do., [illegible]	—	—
37	do.,	Yes,	—	Recurrent hereditary melancholia, with delusions as regards his future.	—	do., [illegible]	—	—

Discharged by order of Lord Lieutenant under the supervision of the Medical Officer, [illegible]

TABLE XI.—PARTICULARS of each case of INSANITY (amongst Prisoners)

[illegible]	Education.	Occupation previous to Conviction.	Crime or Charge.	Date of Conviction (if Convicted).	Sentence (if sentenced).	Date of Reception into a Local Prison

Local Prisons, during Year ended 31st December 1895—*continued.*

No.	Mental Condition on Reception into Local Prison.	Whether previously Insane.	Length of Imprisonment previous to first symptoms of Insanity (in cases originating in Prison).	Form of Insanity.	Recovered in Prison.	Termination of Case. Removed to Asylum. Name of Asylum and Date of Removal.
			LIMERICK (Female).			
[illegible]	Insane,	Yes,	—	Recurrent mania,	–	Limerick, 18. 5. 95,
[illegible]	do.,	do.,	—	do.,	–	Clonmel, 21. 7. 95,
[illegible]	do.,	—	—	do.,	–	do., 1. 8. 95,
[illegible]	do.,	—	—	do.,	–	do., 27. 8. 95,
			LONDONDERRY.			
[illegible]	Sane,	Unknown,	—	Showed no signs of insanity while in prison.	–	Londonderry, 12. 12. 95,
			MOUNTJOY.			
[illegible]	Insane,	Not known,	—	Dementia,	–	Richmond, 14. 1. 95,
[illegible]	do.,	do.,	—	do.,	–	do., 16. 1. 95,
[illegible]	do.,	Yes,	—	Religious mania,	–	do., 18. 4. 95,
[illegible]	do.,	Unknown,	—	Acute mania,	–	do., 15. 4. 95,
[illegible]	do.,	do.,	—	do.,	–	do., 22. 4. 95,
[illegible]	Sane,	do.,	3 months and 27 days.	Dementia,	–	do., 6. 5. 95,
[illegible]	do.,	do.,	18 days,	do.,	–	do., 6. 5. 95,
[illegible]	do.,	do.,	4 months and 9 days,	Melancholia,	–	do., 27. 6. 95,
[illegible]	Insane,	do.,	—	Dementia,	–	do., 24. 9. 95,
[illegible]	do.,	do.,	—	do.,	–	do., 23. 11. 95,
			SLIGO.			
[illegible]	Insane,	Yes,	—	Suicidal mania,	–	Dundrum, 9. 2. 95,
[illegible]	do.,	do.,	—	Melancholia,	–	I. Sligo, 28. 7. 95, II. Dundrum, [illegible]

TABLE XI.—PARTICULARS of each case of INSANITY (amongst Prisoners) in

Age on Admission (if known).	Education.	Occupation previous to Conviction.	Crime or Charge.	Date of Conviction (if Convicted).	Sentence (if sentenced).	Date of Removal from a Local Prison.	[illegible]
			TRALEE.				
37	R.W.	Servant, .	Murder, ...	7. 12. [illegible]	To be detained in custody as a Criminal Lunatic until Her Majesty's pleasure be known.	12. 5. [illegible]	[illegible]
			TULLAMORE.				
[illegible]	Ill.	Labourer, .	Larceny, ...	[illegible]	1 c. m. h. l., . . .	[illegible]	[illegible]
			WATERFORD.				
[illegible]	Ill.	Begging, .	Stealing a horse, . .	—	—	[illegible]	[illegible]

Local Prisons, during Year ended 31st December, 1895—*continued.*

No.	Mental Condition on Reception into a Local Prison.	Whether previously Insane.	Length of Imprisonment previous to first symptoms of Insanity (in cases originating in Prison).	Form of Insanity.	Termination of Case.			
					Recovered in Prison.	Removed to Asylum. Name of Asylum and Date of Removal.	Died in Prison, with Date.	[illegible] in Prison.
				TRALEE.				
[illegible]	Quite sane,	No,	—	Puerperal insanity,	—	Dundrum, [illegible]	—	—
				TULLAMORE.				
[illegible]	Insane,	Yes,	—	Acute mania, recurrent,	—	Maryborough, [illegible]	—	—
				WATERFORD.				
[illegible]	Insane,	Not known,	—	Dementia with delusions,	—	Waterford, [illegible]	—	—
[illegible]	do.,	do.,	—	Acute homicidal mania,	—	do., [illegible]	—	—
[illegible]	do.,	Yes,	—	Puerperal and hysterical insanity,	—	do., [illegible]	—	—
[illegible]	do.,	do.,	—	Dementia with delusions,	—	do., [illegible]	—	—
[illegible]	do.,	do.,	—	Dementia,	—	do., [illegible]	—	—
[illegible]	do.,	Not known,	—	Moral insanity,	—	do., [illegible]	—	—
[illegible]	do.,	do.,	—	Melancholia with paroxysms of acute mania,	—	do., [illegible]	—	—
[illegible]	do.,	do.,	—	Puerperal and delusional,	—	Kilkenny, [illegible]	—	—
				WEXFORD.				
[illegible]	Insane,	Cannot say,	—	Mania,	—	Enniscorthy, [illegible]	—	—
[illegible]	do.,	do.,	—	Dementia,	—	do., [illegible]	—	—

TABLE XII.—RETURN of RESTRAINTS, PRISON OFFENCES, and

(As required by section 15

(See paragraph 93 of Report

Prisons.	Number of Cases of Restraint. Irons (Hand-cuffs.)		Muffs and Straps or Strait Jackets.		Prison Punishments. Punishment Cells.		Dietary Punishment.		Deprivation of Marks or Privilege.		(a) Total number of Prisoners punished.	
Total M. & F., .	2		105		143		5,285		763		3,810	
Larger Prisons.	M.	F.	M.	F.	M.	F.	M.	F.	M.	F.	M.	F.
Armagh, . .	–	–	8	–	12	12	168	8	30	9	105	18
Belfast, . .	–	–	18	6	6	1	841	183	149	47	679	183
Castlebar, . .	–	–	2	–	–	–	89	7	–	–	90	7
Clonmel, . .	–	–	5	–	1	–	101	–	5	–	57	–
Cork Male, . .	–	–	4	–	20	–	478	–	81	–	474	–
Cork Female, .	–	–	–	8	–	–	–	184	–	63	–	219
Dundalk, . .	1	–	8	–	2	–	98	–	81	–	65	–
Galway, . .	–	–	–	1	2	–	62	19	4	8	48	11
Grangegorman, .	–	–	–	24	–	23	–	98	–	11	–	123
Kilkenny, . .	–	–	1	–	12	–	257	–	73	–	83	–
Kilmainham, . .	–	–	6	–	2	–	198	–	92	–	118	–
Limerick Male, .	–	–	2	–	6	–	237	–	86	–	219	–
Limerick Female, .	–	–	–	7	–	1	–	68	–	8	–	37
Londonderry, .	–	–	–	–	8	9	114	30	–	–	147	23
Mountjoy, . .	1	–	8	–	8	–	107	–	130	–	164	–
Sligo, . .	–	–	6	2	5	–	107	8	68	1	86	6
Tralee, . .	–	–	–	–	–	–	177	7	88	1	107	8
Tullamore, . .	–	–	8	6	10	6	395	14	87	8	218	19
Waterford, . .	–	–	3	1	–	8	48	7	1	–	47	6
Wexford, . .	–	–	2	–	8	–	66	2	2	–	73	3
Minor Prisons.												
Carrick-on-Shannon,	–	–	–	–	–	–	–	–	–	–	–	–
Drogheda, . .	–	–	–	–	–	–	–	–	–	–	–	–
Enniskillen, . .	–	–	–	–	–	–	7	2	–	–	7	2
Mullingar, . .	–	–	–	–	–	–	9	–	1	–	10	–
Omagh, . .	–	–	–	–	3	–	4	3	–	–	6	3
Wicklow, . .	–	–	–	–	–	–	1	–	–	–	1	–
Total, . .	2	–	61	44	96	47	4,710	584	681	182	3,389	690

The total number of individuals placed under restraint as above, was, Males, . 36; Females, . 23; [total] 59

Deduct number of prisoners transferred or committed to two Prisons on the same charge, and counted twice above, . . 9 | –

PUNISHMENTS in LOCAL PRISONS from 1st JANUARY, 1893, to 31st DECEMBER, 1893.
of 40 & 41 Vict., cap. 49.)
of Royal Commission, 1884.)

Number of Prisoners punished.		Total number of Prisoners during the Year. (Columns a & b.)		Prison Offences. Violence.		Escapes and Attempts to Escape.		Idleness.		Other Breaches of Regulations.		Total Offences.		Prisons.
29,451		39,681		77		1		1,628		3,259		5,635		Total M. & F.
M.	F.	M.	F.	M.	F.	M.	F.	M.	F.	M.	F.	M.	F.	Larger Prisons.
743	377	854	830	12	1	–	–	126	1	99	22	231	25	Armagh.
3,574	2,136	9,948	2,319	11	9	–	–	174	117	817	148	008	294	Belfast.
410	118	480	122	–	–	–	–	24	3	44	8	67	6	Castlebar.
664	–	741	–	6	–	–	–	38	–	123	–	167	–	Clonmel.
1,854	–	2,129	–	8	–	–	–	287	–	510	–	785	–	Cork Male.
–	622	–	1,044	–	–	–	–	–	22	–	273	–	295	Cork Female.
547	–	682	–	–	–	–	–	29	–	178	–	207	–	Dundalk.
550	103	686	209	–	2	–	–	26	1	60	16	78	10	Galway.
–	4,119	–	4,225	–	–	–	–	–	14	–	128	–	130	Grangegorman.
591	–	635	–	1	–	–	–	34	–	220	–	259	–	Kilkenny.
3,030	–	3,845	–	1	–	–	–	67	–	259	–	327	–	Kilmainham.
1,142	–	1,332	–	2	–	–	–	168	–	304	–	474	–	Limerick Male.
–	527	–	594	–	7	–	–	–	6	–	60	–	73	Limerick Female.
617	418	664	465	–	–	–	–	90	2	151	29	248	31	Londonderry.
3,143	–	3,408	–	6	–	–	–	87	–	223	–	320	–	Mountjoy.
493	179	559	170	5	5	–	–	26	–	174	14	205	17	Sligo.
366	80	491	85	–	–	1	–	64	2	102	6	167	8	Tralee.
651	221	781	240	5	2	–	–	206	–	211	82	422	84	Tullamore.
308	392	310	402	5	9	–	–	17	5	47	10	69	15	Waterford.
250	71	263	78	4	–	–	–	39	–	40	4	83	4	Wexford.
														Minor Prisons.
104	30	104	30	–	–	–	–	–	–	–	–	–	–	Carrick-on-Shannon.
210	76	219	79	–	–	–	–	–	–	–	–	–	–	Drogheda.
135	47	142	48	–	–	–	–	2	–	5	2	7	2	Enniskillen.
231	102	244	102	–	–	–	–	4	–	9	–	13	–	Mullingar.
223	56	224	58	–	–	–	–	1	–	7	2	8	2	Omagh.
168	20	183	20	–	–	–	–	1	–	–	–	1	–	Wicklow.
27,318	9,867	29,057	10,647	38	19	1	–	1,518	110	3,101	788	4,678	917	Total.
1,017	17	1,028	17	–	–	–	–	–	–	–	–	–	–	
28,363	9,880	30,081	10,620	–	–	–	–	–	–	–	–	–	–	

TABLE XIII.—OFFENCES and COMMITMENTS of JUVENILES, i.e., PRISONERS not exceeding 16 years of age, from 1st January, 1895, to 31st December, 1895, (included in foregoing Tables).

PRISONS.	CONVICTED: At Assizes and Quarter Sessions, Under 12 Years.	At Assizes and Quarter Sessions, 12 and not exceeding 16 Years.	Summarily, Under 12 Years.	Summarily, 12 and not exceeding 16 Years.	By Courts Martial, 12 and not exceeding 16 Years.	Total Convictions, Under 12 Years.	Total Convictions, 12 and not exceeding 16 Years.	Not Convicted and Untried, Under 12 Years.	Not Convicted and Untried, 12 and not exceeding 16 Years.	Total Number of Commitments, Under 12 Years.	Total Number of Commitments, 12 and not exceeding 16 Years.
TOTAL, M. & F.,	2	16	19	221	-	21	237	10	104	31	341
MALES.											
Larger Prisons.											
Armagh,	-	1	-	5	-	-	6	-	3	-	9
Belfast,	-	-	2	10	-	2	12	-	5	2	17
Castlebar,	-	1	1	5	-	1	6	-	3	1	9
Clonmel,	-	-	2	5	-	2	5	-	-	2	5
Cork Male,	-	-	-	11	-	-	11	-	6	-	17
Dundalk,	-	-	1	14	-	1	14	-	-	1	14
Galway,	-	1	1	7	-	1	8	1	3	2	11
Kilkenny,	-	-	-	2	-	-	2	-	2	-	4
Kilmainham,	1	4	-	45	-	1	49	3	39	4	88
Limerick Male,	-	3	1	17	-	1	18	-	16	1	34
Londonderry,	-	-	-	5	-	-	5	-	-	-	5
Mountjoy,	1	3	8	47	-	9	50	-	-	9	50
Sligo,	-	1	-	3	-	-	4	-	2	-	6
Tralee,	-	-	-	5	-	-	5	-	3	-	8
Tullamore,	-	-	-	-	-	-	-	-	3	-	3
Waterford,	-	-	1	6	-	1	6	2	1	3	7
Wexford,	-	-	-	1	-	-	1	-	-	-	1
Minor Prisons.											
Carrick-on-Shannon,	-	-	-	-	-	-	-	-	-	-	-
Drogheda,	-	-	1	-	-	1	-	-	-	1	-
Enniskillen,	-	-	-	-	-	-	-	-	-	-	-
Mullingar,	-	-	1	2	-	1	2	-	1	1	3
Omagh,	-	-	-	-	-	-	-	-	4	-	4
Wicklow,	-	-	-	2	-	-	2	-	-	-	2
Total Males,	2	14	19	193	-	21	207	6	90	27	297
FEMALES.											
Larger Prisons.											
Armagh,	-	-	-	-	-	-	-	-	-	-	-
Belfast,	-	-	-	-	-	-	-	-	-	-	-
Castlebar,	-	-	-	1	-	-	1	-	-	-	1
Cork Female,	-	-	-	1	-	-	1	1	3	1	4
Galway,	-	-	-	2	-	-	2	2	-	2	2
Grangegorman,	-	2	-	19	-	-	21	-	4	-	25
Limerick Female,	-	-	-	1	-	-	1	-	-	-	1
Londonderry,	-	-	-	1	-	-	1	1	3	1	4
Sligo,	-	-	-	1	-	-	1	-	-	-	1
Tralee,	-	-	-	2	-	-	2	-	3	-	5
Tullamore,	-	-	-	-	-	-	-	-	-	-	-
Waterford,	-	-	-	-	-	-	-	-	1	-	1
Wexford,	-	-	-	-	-	-	-	-	-	-	-
Minor Prisons.											
Carrick-on-Shannon,	-	-	-	-	-	-	-	-	-	-	-
Drogheda,	-	-	-	-	-	-	-	-	-	-	-
Enniskillen,	-	-	-	-	-	-	-	-	-	-	-
Mullingar,	-	-	-	-	-	-	-	-	-	-	-
Omagh,	-	-	-	-	-	-	-	-	-	-	-
Wicklow,	-	-	-	-	-	-	-	-	1	-	1
Total Females,	-	2	-	28	-	-	30	4	14	4	44

… on Juvenile Prisoners Committed from the 1st January, 1895, to 31st December, 1895.

Imprisonment for																Total.
[illegible]	[illegible]	[illegible]	[illegible]	[illegible]	[illegible]	[illegible]	[illegible]	[illegible]	[illegible]	[illegible]	[illegible]	[illegible]	[illegible]	[illegible]	[illegible]	
-	1	-	3	1	9	94	87	187	-	8	-	8	15	4	356
MALES.																
[illegible]	[illegible]	[illegible]	[illegible]	[illegible]	[illegible]	[illegible]	[illegible]	[illegible]	[illegible]	[illegible]	[illegible]	[illegible]	[illegible]	[illegible]	[illegible]	[illegible]
-	1	-	3	-	8	83	77	90	-	8	-	8	19	4	293
FEMALES.																
[illegible]	[illegible]	[illegible]	[illegible]	[illegible]	[illegible]	[illegible]	[illegible]	[illegible]	[illegible]	[illegible]	[illegible]	[illegible]	[illegible]	[illegible]	[illegible]	[illegible]
-	-	-	-	1	1	1	10	17	-	-	-	-	-	-	60

TABLE XV.—CONDITION of JUVENILES as to

Prisons.	Education on Committal.							
	Neither Read nor Write.		Read or Read and Write Imperfectly.		Read and Write Well.		Superior Instruction.	
	Under 12 years.	12 and not exceeding 16 years.	Under 12 years.	12 and not exceeding 16 years.	Under 12 years.	12 and not exceeding 16 years.	Under 12 years.	12 and not exceeding 16 years.
Total, M. & F.,	18	120	14	119	9	100	-	1
MALES.								
Armagh,	-	9	-	1	-	5	-	-
Belfast,	-	7	3	3	-	13	-	-
Castlebar,	1	3	-	2	-	5	-	-
Clonmel,	-	2	1	-	-	3	-	-
Cork Male,	-	6	-	1	-	30	-	-
Dundalk,	-	5	-	1	-	-	-	-
Galway,	3	3	-	2	-	6	-	-
Kilkenny,	-	1	-	-	-	3	-	-
Kilmainham,	7	28	3	43	-	15	-	1
Limerick, Male,	-	7	-	4	1	13	-	-
Londonderry,	-	2	-	3	-	-	-	-
Mountjoy,	6	15	2	30	1	4	-	-
Sligo,	-	-	-	4	-	7	-	-
Tralee,	-	3	-	-	-	4	-	-
Tullamore,	-	3	-	1	-	-	-	-
Waterford,	1	3	3	4	-	-	-	-
Wexford,	-	-	-	1	-	-	-	-
Minor Prisons.								
Carrick-on-Shannon,	-	-	-	-	-	-	-	-
Drogheda,	-	4	3	8	-	-	-	-
Enniskillen,	-	-	-	-	-	-	-	-
Mullingar,	1	3	-	1	-	-	-	-
Omagh,	-	3	-	3	-	-	-	-
Wicklow,	-	3	-	1	-	-	-	-
Total Males,	10	89	13	105	8	91	-	1
FEMALES.								
Armagh,	-	-	-	-	-	-	-	-
Belfast,	-	-	-	-	-	-	-	-
Castlebar,	-	1	-	-	-	-	-	-
Cork Female,	-	-	-	-	1	3	-	-
Galway,	8	3	-	-	-	3	-	-
Grangegorman,	-	17	-	7	-	3	-	-
Limerick, Female,	-	-	-	1	-	-	-	-
Londonderry,	-	1	1	3	-	-	-	-
Sligo,	-	-	-	1	-	-	-	-
Tralee,	-	-	-	2	-	3	-	-
Tullamore,	-	-	-	-	-	-	-	-
Waterford,	-	-	-	1	-	-	-	-
Wexford,	-	-	-	-	-	-	-	-
Minor Prisons.								
Carrick-on-Shannon,	-	-	-	-	-	-	-	-
Drogheda,	-	-	-	-	-	-	-	-
Enniskillen,	-	-	-	-	-	-	-	-
Mullingar,	-	-	-	-	-	-	-	-
Omagh,	-	-	-	-	-	-	-	-
Wicklow,	-	1	-	-	-	-	-	-
Total Females,	8	31	1	14	1	9	-	-

EDUCATION and RELIGION in 1895.

Religion.										Prisons.
Protestant Episcopalians of Ireland.		Presbyterians.		Roman Catholics.		Other Religions.		Total.		
Under 16 years.	16 and not exceeding 18 years.	Under 16 years.	16 and not exceeding 18 years.	Under 16 years.	16 and not exceeding 18 years.	Under 16 years.	16 and not exceeding 18 years.	Under 16 years.	16 and not exceeding 18 years.	
3	20	-	3	61	317	-	-	64	340	Total, M. & F.
										MALES.
-	2	-	-	-	6	-	-	-	8	Armagh.
2	2	-	3	-	9	-	-	2	17	Belfast.
-	2	-	-	1	6	-	-	1	8	Castlebar.
-	-	-	-	2	5	-	-	2	5	Clonmel.
-	-	-	-	-	17	-	-	-	17	Cork, Male.
-	-	-	-	-	4	-	-	-	4	Dundalk.
-	-	-	-	2	11	-	-	2	11	Galway.
-	-	-	-	-	4	-	-	-	4	Kilkenny.
1	3	-	-	5	60	-	-	6	63	Kilmainham.
-	-	-	-	1	31	-	-	1	34	Limerick, Male.
-	-	-	-	-	5	-	-	-	5	Londonderry.
-	4	-	-	3	48	-	-	3	52	Mountjoy.
-	-	-	-	-	5	-	-	-	5	Sligo.
-	-	-	-	-	8	-	-	-	8	Tralee.
-	-	-	-	-	3	-	-	-	3	Tullamore.
-	-	-	-	3	8	-	-	3	8	Waterford.
-	-	-	-	-	1	-	-	-	1	Wexford.
										Minor Prisons.
-	-	-	-	-	-	-	-	-	-	Carrick-on-Shannon.
-	-	-	-	3	7	-	-	3	7	Drogheda.
-	-	-	-	-	-	-	-	-	-	Enniskillen.
-	-	-	-	1	6	-	-	1	6	Mullingar.
-	1	-	-	-	5	-	-	-	6	Omagh.
-	-	-	-	-	6	-	-	-	6	Wicklow.
3	18	-	3	27	275	-	-	30	296	Total Males.
										FEMALES.
-	-	-	-	-	-	-	-	-	-	Armagh.
-	-	-	-	-	-	-	-	-	-	Belfast.
-	-	-	-	-	1	-	-	-	1	Castlebar.
-	-	-	-	1	3	-	-	1	3	Cork, Female.
-	-	-	-	2	8	-	-	2	8	Galway.
-	1	-	-	-	25	-	-	-	26	Grangegorman.
-	-	-	-	-	1	-	-	-	1	Limerick, Female.
-	-	-	-	1	3	-	-	1	5	Londonderry.
-	-	-	-	-	1	-	-	-	1	Sligo.
-	-	-	-	-	3	-	-	-	3	Tralee.
-	-	-	-	-	-	-	-	-	-	Tullamore.
-	-	-	-	-	1	-	-	-	1	Waterford.
-	-	-	-	-	-	-	-	-	-	Wexford.
										Minor Prisons.
-	-	-	-	-	-	-	-	-	-	Carrick-on-Shannon.
-	-	-	-	-	-	-	-	-	-	Drogheda.
-	-	-	-	-	-	-	-	-	-	Enniskillen.
-	-	-	-	-	-	-	-	-	-	Mullingar.
-	-	-	-	-	-	-	-	-	-	Omagh.
-	1	-	-	-	-	-	-	-	1	Wicklow.
-	3	-	-	6	42	-	-	6	44	Total Females.

F

TABLE XVI.—RETURN of COMMITTALS, &c., to BRIDEWELLS

BRIDEWELLS.	Number in custody at Unlock on 1st January, 18[illegible].		Number of Prisoners committed during year. On remand and afterwards discharged, committed to larger Prisons under sentence or otherwise disposed of.		Under sentence of 12 Hours.		24 Hours and above 12.		48 Hours and above 24.		72 Hours and above 48.		7 Days and above 72 Hours.	
	M.	F.	M.	F.	M.	F.	M.	F.	M.	F.	M.	F.	M.	F.
Bailieborough,	1	-	71	6	-	-	-	1	14	6	-	-	-	-
Ballina, . .	1	-	17	1	-	-	-	-	8	1	64	15	-	-
Ballinasloe, .	1	-	50	5	-	-	84	5	19	11	71	15	-	-
Bantry, . .	-	-	15	8	-	-	-	-	-	-	-	-	-	-
Cahirciveen, .	1	-	6	2	-	-	1	-	8	-	-	-	-	-
Clifden, . .	8	-	17	9	-	-	15	1	16	8	-	-	-	-
Fermoy. .	4	-	84	23	-	-	16	5	10	8	-	-	-	-
Kilrush. . .	-	-	14	3	1	-	6	-	16	6	-	-	5	-
Letterkenny. .	-	-	1	-	91	4	1	3	-	1	-	-	-	-
Loughrea, .	1	-	25	5	-	-	-	-	5	-	-	-	-	-
Mallow, . .	1	-	61	93	-	-	2	-	6	4	20	-	-	-
New Ross, .	-	-	16	4	-	-	7	1	9	5	-	-	-	-
Newry, . .	1	-	45	7	-	-	8	-	95	5	-	-	6	1
Parsonstown, .	3	-	47	15	-	-	5	1	10	3	1	-	87	14
Queenstown,*.	-	-	42	1	-	-	-	-	-	-	-	-	-	-

and Lock-Up at Ennis during the Year 1893.

Number of direct Committals during year.		Number received on way to larger Prisons.		Number otherwise received.		Total number of Prisoners received.		Greatest number of either sex in custody at any one time during above period.	
M.	F.	M.	F.	M.	F.	M.	F.	M.	F.
43	11	8	1	–	–	37	12	8	3
49	17	46	20	–	–	170	43	6	4
54	27	5	1	–	–	[illegible]	26	4	3
16	4	1	–	1	–	17	5	5	1
27	3	3	3	1	–	[illegible]	4	9	3
45	9	14	1	–	–	[illegible]	10	3	2
[illegible]	[illegible]	55	27	–	–	[illegible]	[illegible]	5	1
40	9	1	2	–	–	41	8	5	3
[illegible]	8	–	–	2	1	[illegible]	6	8	2
[illegible]	4	16	–	1	1	61	6	4	2
[illegible]	27	–	–	–	–	[illegible]	27	8	3
[illegible]	3	5	–	–	–	[illegible]	9	3	3
[illegible]	16	8	1	[illegible]	1	176	15	10	3

TABLE XVII.—RETURN of the STAFF of the undermentioned PRISONS and BRIDEWELLS on 31st December, 1895, including vacancies.

PRISONS.	Male Officers.							Female Officers.				Total.	
	Governors and Deputy Governors.	Chief Warders.	Chaplains.	Surgeons and Apothecaries.	Clerks and Storekeepers.	Warders and Bridewell-keepers.	Other Subordinate Officers.	Superintendents and Deputy Superintendents.	Matrons.	Assistant Matrons and Female Attendants.	Servants.	Male.	Female.
LOCAL PRISONS.													
Armagh,	1	1	3	1	1	11	–	–	1	3	1	19	4
Belfast,	2	1	4	1	3	38	–	–	1	18	2	42	18
Castlebar,	1	1	2	1	–	8	–	–	–	1	–	16	2
Clonmel,	1	1	2	1	1	13	–	–	–	–	1	18	1
Cork, Male,	1	1	4	1	1	21	–	–	–	–	1	31	18
Cork, Female,	–	1			–	3	–	–	1	13	1		
Dundalk,	1	1	3	1	1	10	–	–	–	–	1	17	1
Galway,	1	1	3	1	1	9	–	–	–	3	1	15	2
Grangegorman,*	–	1	3	1	–	8	3	1	1	21	2	13	33
Kilkenny,	1	1	3	1	1	12	–	–	–	–	1	19	1
Kilmainham,	2	1	3	1	1	18	–	–	–	–	1	21	1
Limerick, Male,	1	1	2	2	1	14	–	–	–	–	1	23	1
Limerick, Female,	–	1	2	1	–	3	–	–	–	7	3	6	11
Londonderry,	1	1	3	1	1	15	1	–	1	6	1	21	7
Mountjoy,*	2	1	4	2	1	85	2	–	–	–	–	91	*
Sligo,	1	1	2	1	–	10	–	–	–	3	1	13	3
Tralee,	1	1	2	1	–	8	–	–	–	3	1	14	4
Tullamore,	1	1	2	2	1	11	–	–	1	3	1	17	5
Waterford,	1	1	2	1	–	9	–	–	1	3	1	14	3
Wexford,	1	1	2	2	–	8	–	–	–	3	–	14	3
MINOR PRISONS.													
Carrick-on-Shannon,	–	1	–	–	–	1	–	–	1	–	–	2	1
Drogheda,	–	1	–	–	–	1	–	–	1	–	–	2	1
Enniskillen,	–	1	–	–	–	1	–	–	1	–	–	2	1
Mullingar,	–	1	–	–	–	1	–	–	1	–	–	2	1
Omagh,	–	1	–	–	–	1	–	–	1	–	–	2	1
Wicklow,	–	1	–	–	–	1	–	–	1	–	–	2	1
LOCK-UP.													
Cavan,	–	1	–	–	–	2	–	–	1	–	–	3	1
BRIDEWELLS.													
Bailieborough,	–	–	–	–	–	1	–	–	–	–	–	1	–
Ballina,	–	–	–	–	–	1	–	–	–	–	–	1	–
Ballymahon,	–	–	–	–	–	1	–	–	–	–	–	1	–
Bantry,	–	–	–	–	–	1	–	–	–	1	–	1	1
Cahirciveen,	–	–	–	–	–	1	–	–	–	1	–	1	1
Clifden,	–	–	–	–	–	1	–	–	–	–	–	1	–
Fermoy,	–	–	–	–	–	1	–	–	–	1	–	1	1
Kilrush,	–	–	–	–	–	1	–	–	–	–	–	1	–
Letterkenny,	–	–	–	–	–	1	–	–	–	1	–	1	1
Longford,	–	–	–	–	–	1	–	–	–	–	–	1	–
Mallow,	–	–	–	–	–	1	–	–	–	–	–	1	–
New Ross,	–	–	–	–	–	1	–	–	–	1	–	1	1
Newry,	–	–	–	–	–	1	–	–	–	1	–	1	1
Parsonstown,	–	–	–	–	–	1	–	–	–	–	–	1	–
Youghal,	–	–	–	–	–	1	–	–	–	1	–	1	1
Total, 1895-96,	31	27	48	21	14	265	5	1	14	86	19	471	136
Total, 1894-95,	31	27	46	21	14	244	6	1	14	89	19	461	114

* Some of the officers enumerated in the table shown opposite Grangegorman and Mountjoy are also officers of the Convict Prisons at those places.

TABLE XVIII.—ESCAPES from LOCAL PRISONS and BRIDEWELLS from 1st January, 1895, to 31st December, 1895.

Prisons, &c., from which Escapes were effected.	Initials of Name.	Sex.	Age.	Date.	Offence of which convicted or charged.	Tried or Untried.	Whether confined separately or with others.	Whether retaken or not.
Tralee, . . .	J. N.,	M.	60	28.4.95.	Assault & drunk,	Tried, .	Separately, .	Yes.

TABLE XIX.—WORKS of RECONSTRUCTION, REPAIRS, &c., by Contract and by Prison Labour, during the Year ended 31st December, 1895.

LARGER LOCAL PRISONS.

Prisons.	Labour (Contract or Prison).	Detail of Works.
Armagh, . .	Contract,	General repairs to roof of prison and chapel; fixing new washing troughs with waste pipes, &c., in laundry, female prison; repairing weighbridge; repairing roof of town sergeant's house; taking out joints of stone parapet, front of prison, painting in oil and lead putty, and painting same; whitening ceiling in Governor's office, and removing paper in part; re-ceiling board-room, and papering with sanitary paper; erecting electric bell from male hospital to central hall; raking out the joints outside boundary wall of prison, and pointing same with cement; commencing the building of two new cottages for warders, on ground (prison property) adjoining prison.
Do., . .	Prison, .	Erecting two large sheds roofed with corrugated iron, and eight open sheds roofed with same material, for storage of firewood; flooring 19 cells, No. 1 ward, male wing, with Norway pine; erecting mantel registers in officers' quarters, and close range in chief warder's quarters; erecting a ventilating pipe at gable of male wing; general carpentry, painting, glazing, plumbing, gasfitting, whitewashing, and general repairs to buildings.
Belfast, . .	Contract,	Completing erection of new boundary wall enclosing the ground purchased by the Board at rere of prison; concreting and paving of entrance passage at front gate.
Do., . .	Prison, .	Erecting new wooden van shed; setting new fire grates in various parts of the prison; papering quarters in Governor's house; erecting new photo house; general repairs to carpentry, painting, glazing, plumbing, gasfitting, slating, &c., throughout the prison; fixing wire netting on B wing in male prison.
Castlebar, . .	Contract,	Repairing the roofs of the several buildings; setting new range in Governor's kitchen.
Do., .	Prison, .	Fixing railings round altar in Roman Catholic chapel; fitting up new shelving in storekeepers stores; painting, glazing, whitewashing, and chimney-cleaning done throughout the prison, and keeping in repair all yards, roads, and walks.
Clonmel, . .	Contract,	Erection of flushing barrel in hospital yard; repairing ranges in cook-house and officers' mess; repairing bath and roof in Governor's house; erection of framed sliding door in coal shed; repairing water pipes of prison and warders' cottages; altering and repairing Protestant church.

TABLE XIX.—WORKS of RECONSTRUCTION, REPAIRS, &c.—*continued.*

Prisons.	Labour. (Contract or Prison).	Detail of Works.
Clonmel, . .	Prison, .	Plastering portion of wall in surgery; repairing iron check gate at entrance, and laying flags in kitchen floor at gate quarters; laying 50 yards of concrete kerbing around grass plots in front of office, and making a concrete passage to laundry; building a concrete wall around ashpit, and pebble dashing same; shelving store room in reception; general repairs to painting, glazing, masonry, carpentry, and smithwork throughout the prison.
Cork Male, . .	Contract,	Cementing end wall of Governor's house and repairing part of boundary wall of prison.
Do., . .	Prison, .	Reconstruction of laundry building, and conversion of portion of same into stores; erecting new bath-house at end of right wing of male prison, also new water closets and flush tank in No. 9 yard, by convict labour; erecting eighteen new stone sheds in stone yard, and a locked shed for storing manufactured firewood; putting on new snow boards and repairing old ones on roof of tower and main prison; putting on new skirting on stairs and halls in hospital; fixing up two water closets, and a bath, and lavatory, with a supply of hot and cold water, in officers' quarters, also painting throughout same; renewing concrete paths in exercise yards of No. 9 and 10 sections; making new doorway to No. 10 section exercise yard; repairs to painting, glazing, plumbing, masonry and carpentry throughout the prison.
Cork Female, .	Contract,	Papering and painting chief warder's quarters, and bedroom in matron's quarters; fixing new water supply to closets in hospital, and repairing water pipes; making five new concrete exercise rings; flooring and partitioning room in hospital for an officer's bedroom; flooring and repairing rooms in warders' quarters; repairing and fixing 49 cell windows; repairing ranges and grates of prison; building wall at upper end of field outside the prison.
Do., . .	Prison, .	General repairs to whitewashing, painting, glazing, and to W.C. gear, baths, &c.
Dundalk, . .	Contract,	Repairs to skylights and roof of prison, steam boiler, cooking pans in kitchen, and crank pump.
Do., . .	Prison, .	Covering old disused well at the rere of prison with new flooring, and putting trap door on; general repairs to bells and gas and water pipes; repairs to carpentry, painting, and glazing throughout the prison; painting of woodwork and whitewashing of walls.
Galway, . .	Contract,	New water supply pipe to chief warder's quarters; new water supply pipe to male hospital yard, and repairs to water pipe same yard; new valve reception bath; new supply pipes to two W.C.s, male reception; fixing new water supply pipe, with H.P. cock, to No. 1 bath; the erection, in part, of four warders' cottages.

TABLE XIX.—WORKS OF RECONSTRUCTION, REPAIRS, &c.—*continued.*

Prisons.	Labour (Contract or Prison).	Detail of Works.
Galway, . . .	Prison, . .	New chimney stack over the Governor's office; painting and varnishing woodwork in do.; painting and papering bedroom in Governor's house; papering and painting chief warder's quarters, and fixing new stove; completing coping of laundry wall; removing old laundry at rere of stone yard and forming new doorway; building concrete wall from stone yard gate to boundary wall, and paving space between entrance gates with paving bricks laid on a bed of concrete; removing part of old town prison, and repairing wall from do. to general store; putting down 80 feet of sewer pipes in front of stone sheds for surface drainage, and forming concrete paths in front of stone yard and offices; setting cut stone steps at laundry door and between female prison and garden; building up doorway in male reception, and putting new chimney pots on chimney of male hospital; putting down 8 new grates and concrete hearths in gate quarters, &c.; general repairs to roofs, boilers, heating pipes, &c.; painting woodwork, and whitening walls and ceilings.
Grangegorman, .	Contract,	Whitening ceilings, and painting walls and woodwork of entrance hall; whitening ceilings; colouring walls in corridors, and painting dado and woodwork in main entrance and tower; regilding dials of clock on tower and weather vane; erection of 3 new baths in hospital; also slop-trough and wash-hand basin in surgery; erection of new portable baths, and laying heating pipes to Protestant and R. C. chapels; fixing boilers and ranges in cook house and laundries with new fire blocks and bottoms and front grailings; cleaning flues of drying closets in convict and local laundry, and windows in front buildings.
Do., . .	Prison, . .	Erection of 6 new ventilators on roof of new hall, and making fresh air inlet on ground floor at end of hall; closing old pattern ventilators on side walls; carpentry and masonry work in connection with 3 new baths in hospital; erection of galvanized framing and wire lattice on balconies and staircase of new hall; and new shelving and case of drawers in surgery; repairs to carpentry, plumbing, gas-fitting, glazing, and bell-hanging; whitening walls and painting woodwork.
Kilkenny, . .	Contract,	Building of new wall at end of warders cottages; erection of iron wicket at side of entrance gate to cottages, and plastering of adjoining wall in cement; fixing gunmetal gauge-cock and test-cock to steam boiler in cook house, and repairing water pipes in reception; general repairs to crank pump; papering dining rooms in warders' cottages, and repairing gas meter of same; repairs to roof of Governor's house, bursts and leakages in water pipes, locks; painting woodwork, and papering walls.
Do., .	Prison, .	Removing old grate in main hall and setting new stove; repairing and fixing new sashes and frames in Governor's office, and new gate; erection of 5 stone breaking sheds, including new roof, slates, &c.; making new frames for mat-making; general repairs to pumps, locks, gas, and water pipes, taps, &c.; cleaning, whitening, and painting of 7 warders' cottages; general repairs to woodwork, &c., and mess room; painting, colouring, and whitening of officers quarters, cells, corridors, &c.
Kilmainham, . .	Contract,	Completing erection of chief warder's cottage; repairing boiler in A wing; putting twelve windows into new reception cells, and two large windows in corridor of same; repairing roof of prison and Governor's house; removing iron gate in front of prison cottages, and fixing it in another position; repairing electric bells to hospital, &c.; removing old boiler in A wing and substituting a new one.
Do., .	Prison, . .	Construction of W. C. in new reception ward; enlarging of 30 windows in reception cells and passages, and 13 in B wing for the admission of more light and air; enclosing of Governor's garden, and putting up entrance door with check gate, erecting stairs therefrom to Governor's house; general repairs to painting, glazing, plumbing, gas-fitting, and carpentry, &c., throughout the prison.

TABLE XIX.—WORKS of RECONSTRUCTION, REPAIRS, &c.—*continued.*

Prisons.	Labour (Contract or Prison).	Detail of Works.
Limerick Male, .	Contract,	Alteration of chimney in Governor's house.
Do., . .	Prison, .	Removing old roof of tower, putting on new one, and covering same with lead; removing, repairing, and re-erecting balustrade on tower roof; erecting new shed in wood yard for storage of firewood; laying new concrete footpaths in front of prison and [illegible] exercise yard; removing walls around reception and hospital yards and [illegible] of tower; concrete coping 150 yards of boundary wall; [illegible] heating apparatus in reception, and repairing heating furnaces in main hall and F wing; repairing W. C. in chief warder's quarters, and enlarging window of same; general repairs to buildings, including painting, glazing, slating, whitewashing, and plumbing, &c.
Limerick Female, .	Contract,	Repairs to roofs of assistant matrons' quarters; putting up new No. [illegible] Stanley range in cook house; plastering where defective and whitewashing the following yards, viz.:—pump yard, hard labour yard, and laundry yard; whitewashing chief warder's yard, hall yard, and interior of laundry; colouring wall at front entrance adjoining city courthouse; coping with cement the boiler wall, also walls in laundry, hall, and pump yards; forming new ironing room in laundry; erecting new stove; constructing new stairs from laundry proper to ironing room; painting with naphtha all eave gutters, down pipes, and bars of cell windows throughout the prison; repairing four windows in Protestant church, and laying out with clay and grass seeds both pump and hall yards; forming new concrete floor over drying house in laundry; repairing broken band in heating apparatus; [illegible] the cupola on tower over Protestant church; fixing up gutters and down pipes on married quarters' closet; pointing chimney shaft over chief warder's quarters; fixing up gutters on south side of church and clearing away all vegetable matter on outer walls.
Do., . .	Prison, .	General repairs to gas and water pipes; painting, glazing, and whitewashing throughout prison.
Londonderry, .	Contract,	Opening out and fixing in three new windows and frames in male hospital; re-setting range and new boiler in chief warder's quarters, and keeping in repair electric bells, roofs, eave gutters, and down pipes; also of gas and water pipes.
Do., . .	Prison, .	Casing in electric bell wires; fixing up new scullery trough in Governor's house; making and fixing new window frame and sash in shoemakers' shop; casing steam boiler (female prison) with patent composition; enlarging eleven cells (men's prison); repairing 35 window sills; fixing in new fire grate (female officers' quarters); repairs to windows, furniture, yards, roads, and walks.
Mountjoy (Local), .	Contract,	Fixing up lightning conductors to large chimney stacks and air shafts.
Do., . .	Prison, .	Putting down 450 yards of concrete paths in exercise rings; removing rubbish and levelling ground; putting additional floor lights at end of central hall for lighting passages in basement, and putting additional ventilators in ditto; setting new boilers in cook house and repairing furnaces; cleaning and repairing furnaces of heating pipes, baths, &c.; repairing roofs of work sheds; repairing and cleaning roads, paths, &c.; cleaning and whitewashing cells and corridors of prison, and painting woodwork and iron work.
Sligo, . . .	Contract,	Repairs to roof of prison damaged by storm; repairs to water pipes in yard of Governor's house and in cell yard. Altering water supply to new cottages outside prison; stripping and whitewashing walls in chief warders' quarters; rebuilding scullery of Governor's house; converting old day room of female prison into two new cells, bath, and boiler rooms; re-[illegible] walls of new prison cottages; cleaning and colouring interior of old prison cottage; repairs to roof of [illegible]; repairs to tanks in male bathroom and laundry; alterations to gas fittings in offices and supplying gas fittings to two warders' rooms; setting new range in [illegible] kitchen.

TABLE XIX.—WORKS of RECONSTRUCTION, REPAIRS, &c.—*continued.*

Prisons.	Labour. (Contract or Prison).	Detail of Works.
Sligo, . . .	Prison, .	Papering two rooms in Governor's house, and painting hall; colouring and painting Protestant and Roman Catholic chapels; building up doorway in clerk's office and opening new doorway from lavatory to passage; boarding 21 cells in central block; flagging three rings in exercise yards; general repairs to painting and whitewashing throughout the prison.
Tralee, . .	Contract,	Taking down projecting gas fittings and fixing up gas shields in male and female hospitals and rooms in tower; taking down projecting bell pulls and fixing up flush ones in same rooms; repairing hot-water tank and pipes in mess; repairing heating pipes at male prison, boiler and [illegible] hot water pipes at Governor's quarters; fixing up new hot water cistern and pipes in warders' [illegible]; taking down and cleaning out gas fittings in male prison; fixing up new electric bell from hall of male prison to chief warder's quarters, and new lead-lined cistern to supply W.C. in [illegible] yard; taking down old [illegible] gas fittings of mess room, and replacing with new fittings; removing gas meter and connecting pipes; repairing gas mains at back of prison.
Do., .	Prison, .	Putting new cement copings on inside boundary walls; fitting up shelving and racks in three warders' cottages; fixing up new flushing barrel, complete, on tower from warders' cottages; making new hot water cistern for mess; filling up and paving 23 stone sheds; laying new concrete floor in passage to cook-house; painting and lime-washing the entire prison; general repairs to eave gutters, roofs, buildings, glazing, &c.; repairs to locks and keys.
Tullamore, . .	Contract,	Supplying and erecting soil pipe to W.C. in Governor's house; repairs to burst pipes and gas connection in chief warder's quarters; repairs to burst pipes in hospital, and to hot water pipes of prison; laying of metal pipe (and sluice valve) from town main to prison, and water pipes in prison and to warders' cottages.
Do., .	Prison, .	Alterations to mess room and stores; removing old stairs and erecting two new doors; putting down new floors and plastering walls and ceilings; making and fixing new shelving and bins in provision store; repairing lead gutters and re-slating roofs where damaged; opening and closing trenches for water pipes; roofing female reception with new slate roof, building up walls, in part, to roof, and fixing wood ceiling; repairing and glazing windows of prison; removing flags from seven cells, and putting down boarded floors; fixing six shutters to hospital building; repairs to 24 plank beds; new window to female padded cell; painting and whitewashing prison.
Waterford, .	Contract,	Fitting fanlights in windows at ends of male and female prisons; putting up new ballcock in large tank; fixing up new laundry stove and gas meter; connecting the flushing barrel of kitchen with town water, by lead pipe from kitchen supply; putting up bars on closet windows; repairs to hot and cold water pipes throughout the prison.
Do., . .	Prison, .	Erection of 23 stone sheds; painting and glazing the glass roofs on male and female prisons; painting in distemper the walls of officers' mess and quarters; putting up new shelves in female clothing store; erection of new shed over ladders in hospital yard; repairs to carpentry, painting, glazing, whitewashing; repairs to locks and gas pipes, &c., throughout male and female prison hospitals, &c.
Wexford, .	Contract,	Setting of new marble mantel with register grate in Governor's house; setting of cooking range in married warders' quarters; repairs to water pipes, closet cisterns, and taps, chimney stacks and roofs of male prison, and lawn mower; clearing of [illegible] grounds.

TABLE XIX.—WORKS of RECONSTRUCTION, REPAIRS, &c.—*continued.*

MINOR PRISONS.

Minor Prisons.	Labour (Contract or Prison).	Detail of Works.
Wexford, . .	Prison, .	Removing of old flooring from 22 cells in male prison, and putting down new floors, including joists, tassels, flooring boards, skirting, &c.; fixing protection netting around hall of male prison, and altering the old netting of corridors; erection of new shed for storing timber, &c.; opening old wells, 10 in number, and recovering them securely with flags, &c.; general repairs to roofs, doors, windows, &c.; painting of woodwork and colouring of walls, &c.
Carrick-on-Shannon,	Contract,	Slight repairs to roof of male prison after storm; general repairs to ceilings in the prison; repairs to skylights of workshop, and painting same; cleaning outlets of main sewers in connection with the prison; removing old tread mill and house in connection with it.
Do., . .	Prison, .	Nil.
Drogheda, . .	Contract,	New stove pipe in range in cooking kitchen; repairs to lead pipes; new W. C. in chief warder's quarters; pointing of boundary wall in cement both sides; coping 51 yards of wall with cement; dashing of 40 yards of wall in front of prison; new ballcock arrangement to W. C. in male prison; erection of new heating boiler, male prison.
Do., . .	Prison, .	General limewashing of prison, and walls of yard; painting of iron and woodwork of prison doors, gates, and all outside doors.
Enniskillen, . .	Contract,	Repairs to roof of male and female prisons, damaged by recent storm; improving water supply to chief warder's quarters; repairs to burst water pipes; setting two new gulley traps; altering gas meter and supply pipes; erection of new range in gate warder's kitchen, and boarding two bedrooms in his quarters; papering and whitening ceiling of sitting room in chief warder's quarters.
Do., . .	Prison, .	Erection of two wooden sheds for stone breaking; whitening ceiling and colouring walls of gate warder's quarters; repairs to burst water pipes in female prison after recent frost; whitewashing, painting, glazing, and similar repairs executed throughout the prison.
Mullingar, . .	Contract,	Sundry repairs to roof and chimneys; fixing 12 yards eave gutter; fixing 11 feet new flue pipe in laundry and kitchen; repairing two doors, and pump and lead pipe; fixing 5 new valves in water tanks; altering heating system, and fixing five pieces hot water pipe and two bends; building up a window in garden wall; erecting arch in front of heating boiler; taking out 51 lineal yards of joints in flagging of platform, and pointing with cement; laying down 17½ superficial yards of tiles in kitchen at gate quarters.
Do., . .	Prison, .	Whitewashing walls and ceilings of prison cells, corridors, stores, and officers' quarters; cleaning and varnishing chapel doors, yard doors, entrance gate and doors; painting cell doors and skirtings; glazing windows where necessary; taking down two disused buildings.
Omagh, . .	Contract,	General repairs to roofs, eave gutters, &c., damaged by storm; repairs to gas pipes in male prison, chief warder's, and warders' quarters; repairs to kitchen range and water pipes burst by frost in stone yard, heating house, male and female prisons; fitting up new holland blinds to glass windows in chief warder's quarters; fitting up new top to stove for cooking prisoners' food; removing flagging from living room in warders' quarters, and fitting in new boarded floor instead.

TABLE XIX.—WORKS OF RECONSTRUCTION, REPAIRS, &c.—*continued.*

MINOR PRISONS.

Minor Prisons.	Labour (Contract or Prison.)	Detail of Work.
Omagh, . .	Prison, .	Repairing kitchen stairs and two bed room doors, and papering two rooms in chief warder's quarters; painting one room in warders' quarters; replacing broken flags in hall of male prison by new ones; and putting up 1[illegible] feet of eave gutters on same building; building up cavities in walls of tread mill house from which machinery had been removed, and repairing breach in wall at water tank; painting and pebble-dashing part of the walls in exercise yards, and at chapel steps; repairs to roofs of stone sheds and gate house; cutting out damaged heating pipes in chapel, and replacing them by new ones; glazing windows, and general painting and whitewashing.
Wicklow, . .	Contract,	New roof to coach house; new pipe to stove in clothing store; new ceiling to corridor of male prison; new ventilator to male prison; new water supply pipe and sink to kitchen; plumbing repairs to supply pipe of heating apparatus, and new stop cock; cleaning prison sewer and making a new pipe sewer from boundary wall to main sewer.
Do., . .	Prison, .	General limewashing of prison, walls, yards, closets, &c.; painting iron and woodwork of gates, doors, &c.

BRIDEWELLS.

Bailieboro', . .	Contract,	Papering of keeper's dining room and office.
Belfast, . .	Contract,	Repairing the roof of.
Ballinasloe, . .	Contract,	Putting on new valves on pump, and clearing the well out; cleaning eave gutters and down pipes, and repairing valley of roof; cleaning three privies and sewer leading to female yard; painting windows inside and out, bar doors, gates, and stonework in cells; colouring and painting five apartments belonging to keeper; also doors, windows, shutters, and skirtings of same; painting and repairing eave shoots and down pipes; painting entrance gate and office door, &c.
Clifden, . .	Contract,	Putting in 8 new bars in 4 cell windows; repairing chimney and erecting chimney pot; sundry repairs to roof and doors; repairs to entrance gate and door of W. C.; putting in new window, and papering keeper's sitting room.
Newry, . . .	Contract,	Papering keeper's quarters; and repairing bell at entrance gate.

TABLE XX.—RETURNS SHOWING EMPLOYMENT OF PRISONERS IN LOCAL PRISONS AND ESTIMATED VALUE OF THEIR EARNINGS.

(As required by 40–41 Vict., cap. 49, section 16).

(A.) Return showing the Prisons in which each Description of Employment has been carried on during the Year.

Description of Employment.	Prisons in which carried on.	Total Number of Prisons.
I.—Non-productive, ...	—	[illegible]
II.—In Manufactures:—		
Brushmaking, ...	Mountjoy, ...	1
Knitting and needleworking, .	Belfast, Castlebar, Cork F., Grangegorman, Limerick F., Londonderry, Sligo, Tullamore, Waterford, Drogheda.	10
Matmaking, plaiting, and other work connected therewith.	Belfast, Clonmel, Cork M., Dundalk, Galway, Kilkenny, Limerick M., Londonderry, Mountjoy, Sligo, Wexford.	11
Picking or teasing oakum, hair, &c.	All prisons except *Cork F. and Limerick F.*,	24
Sackmaking, ...	Kilmainham, Mountjoy, Tullamore, . . .	3
Shoemaking, ...	Armagh, Belfast, Kilkenny, Limerick M., Mountjoy, Tullamore, Wexford.	7
Knitting, ...	Armagh, Belfast, Limerick M., Londonderry, Sligo, Tullamore.	6
Stonebreaking, ...	Armagh, Belfast, Castlebar, Cork M., Dundalk, Galway, Kilkenny, Kilmainham, Limerick M., Londonderry, Mountjoy, Sligo, Tralee, Tullamore, Waterford, Wexford, Drogheda, Enniskillen, Mullingar, Omagh.	20
Tailoring, ...	Armagh, Belfast, Kilkenny, Tralee, Waterford, Wexford.	6
Washing, not including prisoners' clothing.	Armagh, Belfast, Castlebar, Clonmel, Cork F., Galway, Grangegorman, Limerick F., Londonderry, Sligo, Tralee, Tullamore, Waterford, Wexford.	14
Woodcutting, ...	Armagh, Belfast, Clonmel, Cork M., Dundalk, Galway, Kilkenny, Kilmainham, Limerick M., Londonderry, Sligo, Tralee, Tullamore, Waterford, Wexford, Drogheda, Enniskillen, Mullingar, Omagh.	19
Carpet cleaning, . . .	Belfast, Galway, Londonderry, ...	3
Linen cutting, . . .	Belfast, ...	1
Weaving, ...	Mountjoy, ...	1
Tinsmithing, ...	Mountjoy, Waterford, ...	2
Carpentry, ...	Limerick M., Tralee, Waterford, ...	3

(A.)—continued—Return showing the Prisons in which each Description of Employment has been carried on during the Year.

Description of Employment.	Prisons in which carried on.	Total Number of Prisons.
III.—In Buildings :—		
Bricklayers or masons, . .	Armagh, Belfast, Clonmel, Cork M., Galway, Kilkenny, Kilmainham, Limerick M., Londonderry, Tralee, Waterford, Omagh.	12
Carpenters or joiners, . .	Armagh, Belfast, Clonmel, Cork M., Dundalk, Galway, Kilkenny, Kilmainham, Limerick M., Londonderry, Sligo, Tralee, Tullamore, Waterford, Omagh.	15
Labourers, ...	All prisons except *Cork F., Grangegorman, Limerick F., Sligo, Waterford, Wexford, Carrick, Drogheda, Enniskillen, and Wicklow.*	28
Painters and glaziers, . .	All prisons except *Cork F., Grangegorman, Carrick.*	35
Plasterers.	Belfast, Clonmel, Kilmainham, Omagh. . .	4
Plumbers and gasfitters, . .	Belfast, Cork M., Kilmainham, . . .	3
Smiths, ...	Belfast, Clonmel, Cork M., Galway, Kilkenny, and Omagh.	6
Whitewashers, ...	All prisons, ...	38
Stonebreaking for concreting, &c.	Londonderry, Mountjoy, ...	2
IV.—In the ordinary service of the Prisons :—		
Cleaning and jobbing work in and about the prisons, &c.	All prisons, ...	38
Cooking for the prisoners, . .	All prisons except *Grangegorman, Carrick, Enniskillen, Mullingar, and Omagh.*	33
Nursing and attending sick prisoners, children, &c.	Armagh, Belfast, Clonmel, Cork M., Cork F., Galway, Kilmainham, Limerick M., Limerick F., Londonderry, Mountjoy, Sligo, Tralee, Tullamore, Waterford, Drogheda, Omagh.	17
Pumping water for the prisons,	Castlebar, Clonmel, Cork M., Dundalk, Kilkenny, Limerick M., Tullamore, Waterford, Wexford, Mullingar, Wicklow.	11
Repairing all kinds of prison clothing.	All prisons, ...	38
Repairing all kinds of prison shoes.	Armagh, Belfast, Castlebar, Clonmel, Cork M., Dundalk, Galway, Kilkenny, Kilmainham, Limerick M., Londonderry, Mountjoy, Sligo, Tralee, Tullamore.	15
Repairing all kinds of prison utensils.	Belfast, Clonmel, Cork M., ...	3
Making prison furniture, . .	Belfast, Clonmel, Kilkenny, Kilmainham, Londonderry, Tullamore, Waterford.	7
Washing prisoners' clothing, .	All prisons except *Limerick M., and Mountjoy.*	36
Gardening, ...	Armagh, Belfast, Cork F., Dundalk, Galway, Londonderry, Sligo, Tralee, and Enniskillen.	9
Baking for prisoners, . .	Cork M., ...	1
Upholsterers.	Kilmainham.	1

(B.)—*Separate Returns from each Prison.*

ARMAGH PRISON.

Return by the Governor, showing the employment of the Prisoners and value of their Earnings during the year ended 31st March, 1896.

Description of Employment.	Daily Average Number of Prisoners (for working days of the year).			Value of Prisoners' Labour.	Total.
	M.	F.	Total.	£ s. d.	£ s. d.
In Manufactures:—					
Picking or teasing oakum, hair, &c.,	11·41	8·1	19·61	16 3 0	
Shoemaking,	·11	—	·11	—	
Knitting,	·16	—	·16	—	
Sack-making,	18·11	—	18·11	70 11 0	
Tailoring,	·10	6·3	6·40	1 8 4	
Washing, not including prisoners' clothing,	—	1·88	1·88	0 0 5	
Woodcutting,	16·64	—	16·64	44 14 4	
Total,	44·23	16·00	60·6		140 12 9
In Buildings:—					
Bricklayers or masons,	·17	—	·17	8 10 0	
Carpenters or joiners,	·15	—	·15	6 15 0	
Labourers,	1·76	—	1·76	62 5 0	
Painters and glaziers,	·29	—	·28	7 18 10	
Whitewashers,	·30	·1	·32	8 11 0	
Total,	2·31	·1	2·31		91 16 6
In the ordinary service of the Prison:—					
Cleaning and jobbing work in and about the prison and prison yard and buildings (exclusive of building work of any kind),	4·34	1·50	4·97	44 10 0	
Cooking for the prisoners,	3·63	—	3·63	106 4 0	
Nursing and attending sick prisoners,	—	1·1	1·1	34 19 4	
Repairing all kinds of prison clothing,	·07	0·04	0·11	178 12 0	
Repairing all kinds of prison shoes,	·75	—	·75	14 9 0	
Washing prisoners' clothing,	—	6·07	6·07	73 7 0	
Gardening,	·22	—	·22	4 4 0	
Total,	9·61	14·24	22·35		482 4 0
Non-effective:—					
Sick,	3·05	·96	3·01	—	
Under punishment,	·16	·04	·21	—	
Unemployed:—					
Awaiting trial,	1·83	3·34	5·17	—	
Debtors,	·15	—	·15	—	
Others, &c.,	·01	·34	·35	—	
Total,	4·61	5·40	7·9	—	
Grand Total,	59·45	25·21	81·65	—	653 18 4

BELFAST PRISON.

RETURN by the GOVERNOR, showing the employment of the Prisoners and value of their Earnings during the year ended 31st March, 1896.

Description of Employment.	Daily Average Number of Prisoners (for working days of the year). M.	F.	Total.	Value of Prisoners' Labour. £ s. d.	Total. £ s. d.
In Manufactures :—					
Knitting and needleworking,	—	25·41	25·41	114 10 9	
Mat-making, plaiting, and other work connected therewith,	75·51	—	75·51	178 7 4	
Picking or teasing oakum, hair, &c.,	47·99	19·51	67·39	130 1 10	
Shoemaking,	5·09	—	5·09	157 11 9	
Smithing,	1·03	—	1·03	37 17 6	
Stonebreaking,	65·21	—	65·21	223 10 2	
Tailoring,	5·90	—	5·90	132 11 9	
Washing, not including prisoners' clothing,	—	6·43	6·43	66 3 11	
Woodcutting,	1·90	—	1·90	9 16 7	
Linen cutting,	—	17·17	17·17	91 16 7	
Carpet cleaning,	16·99	—	16·99	312 2 5	
Total,	181·90	71·07	252·71		1,443 18 10
In Buildings :—					
Bricklayers or masons,	·20	—	·20	7 11 6	
Carpenters or joiners,	1·70	—	1·70	44 7 8	
Labourers,	21·99	—	21·99	450 0 0	
Painters and glaziers,	·91	—	·91	35 17 6	
Plasterers,	·30	—	·30	7 11 9	
Plumbers and gasfitters,	1·01	—	1·01	23 4 1	
Smiths,	·40	—	·40	12 16 3	
Whitewashers,	·11	—	·11	2 16 7	
Total,	26·63	—	26·63		600 19 7
In the ordinary service of the Prison :—					
Cleaning and jobbing work in and about the prison and prison yard, and buildings (exclusive of building work of any kind),	11·44	8·14	19·58	816 17 7	
Cooking for the prisoners,	6·10	—	6·10	177 8 7	
Nursing and attending sick prisoners,	·63	2·16	2·74	49 1 8	
Repairing all kinds of prison clothing,	8·28	6·12	14·38	709 17 2	
Repairing all kinds of prison shoes,	3·77	—	3·77	97 16 2	
Repairing all kinds of prison utensils,	·27	—	·27	7 0 3	
Stoking prison furnaces,	1·21	—	1·21	26 0 7	
Washing prisoners' clothing,	·50	7·51	8·01	189 3 8	
Gardening,	·49	—	·49	8 6 7	
Total,	34·99	24·23	64·74		1,115 6 10
Non-effective :—					
Sick,	7·66	·26	7·97	—	
Under punishment,	1·24	·51	1·75	—	
Unemployed :—					
Awaiting trial,	12·99	2·16	15·18	—	
Debtors,	·41	—	·41	—	
First class misdemeanants,	—	·40	·40	—	
Others, &c.,	24·57	11·60	36·16	—	
Total,	40·73	15·01	56·66	—	
Grand Total,	[illegible]	111·16	[illegible]	—	3,375 14 5

CASTLEBAR PRISON.

Return by the Governor, showing the employment of the Prisoners and value of their Earnings during the year ended 31st March, 1896.

Description of Employment.	Daily Average Number of Prisoners (for working days of the year).			Value of Prisoners' Labour.	Total.
	M.	F.	Total.	£ s. d.	£ s. d.
In Manufactures:—					
Knitting and needleworking,	—	6·22	6·22	45 15 9	
Picking or teasing oakum, hair, &c.,	6·36	—	7·39	—	
Stonebreaking,	11·21	—	11·21	6 9 6	
Washing, not including prisoners' clothing,	—	·70	·70	0 5 10	
Total,	11·29	6·12	17·71		55 11 4
In Buildings:—					
Painters and Glaziers,	·07	—	·07	2 2 11	
Whitewashers,	·18	—	·18	4 10 11	
Total,	·25	—	·25		6 13 10
In the ordinary service of the Prison:—					
Cleaning and jobbing work in and about the prison and prison yard and buildings (exclusive of building work of any kind),	3·31	·34	3·65	67 4 7	
Cooking for the prisoners,	1·	—	1·	55 1 6	
Pumping water for the service of the prison only,	·50	—	·50	9 9 6	
Repairing all kinds of prison clothing,	·25	1·50	1·75	33 9 10	
Repairing all kinds of prison shoes,	·10	—	·10	1 17 10	
Washing prisoners' clothing,	—	1·55	1·55	20 7 1	
Total,	5·16	3·39	8·45		170 8 3
Non-effective:—					
Sick,	·78	·06	·84	—	
Under punishment,	·12	·03	·15	—	
Unemployed:—					
Awaiting trial,	3·12	·09	3·21	—	
Others, &c.,	1·28	1·16	2·44	—	
Total,	5·30	1·34	6·64	—	
Grand Total,	25·	8·86	33·86	—	[illegible] 13 7

CLONMEL (MALE) PRISON.

Return by the Governor, showing the employment of the Prisoners and value of their Earnings during the year ended 31st March, 1896.

Description of Employment.	Daily Average Number of Prisoners (for working days of the year).	Value of Prisoners' Labour.	Total.
	M.	£ s. d.	£ s. d.
In Manufactures:—			
Mat-making, plaiting and other work connected therewith,	·7	5 6 7	
Picking or teasing oakum, hair, &c.,	9·74	—	
Washing, not including prisoners' clothing,	4·	124 12 7	
W[illegible],	9·94	57 9 6	
Total,	24·59		164 10 10

CLONMEL (MALE) PRISON—*continued.*

RETURN by the GOVERNOR, showing the employment of the Prisoners and value of their Earnings during the year ended 31st March, 1896.

Description of Employment.	Daily Average Number of Prisoners (for working days of the year).	Value of Prisoners' Labour.	Total.
	m.	£ s. d.	£ s. d.
In Buildings :—			
Bricklayers or masons,	·02	0 14 0	
Carpenters or joiners,	·1	1 4 6	
Painters and glaziers,	·25	7 8 8	
Plasterers,	·04	1 8 8	
Smiths,	·01	0 10 8	
Whitewashers,	·04	1 8 8	17 13 3
Total,	·31		
In the ordinary service of the Prison :—			
Cleaning and jobbing work in and about the prison and prison yard and buildings (exclusive of building work of any kind),	10·62	190 11 5	
Cooking for the prisoners,	5·77	65 4 5	
Nursing and attending sick prisoners,	·15	9 17 0	
Pumping water for the service of the prison only,	9·65	140 11 9	
Repairing all kinds of prison clothing,	1·45	53 11 8	
Repairing all kinds of prison shoes,	·71	25 11 8	
Repairing all kinds of prison utensils,	·34	10 8 0	
Picking prison furniture,	1·01	25 11 6	
Washing prisoners' clothing,	5·	87 6 6	619 13 3
Total,	39·35		
Non-effective :—			
Sick,	1·41	—	
Under punishment,	·25	—	
Unemployed :—			
Awaiting trial,	1·9	—	
Debtors,	·01	—	
First class misdemeanants,	1·47	—	
Others, &c.,	2·15	—	
Total,	5·04	—	
Grand Total,	65·65	—	787 15 8

CORK (MALE) PRISON.

RETURN by the GOVERNOR, showing the employment of the Prisoners and value of their Earnings during the year ended 31st March, 1896.

Description of Employment.	Daily Average Number of Prisoners (for working days of the year).	Value of Prisoners' Labour.	Total.
	m.	£ s. d.	£ s. d.
In Manufactures :—			
Matmaking, plaiting, and other work connected therewith,	30·19	60 14 8	
Picking or teasing oakum, hair, &c.,	78·31	14 10 7	
Stonebreaking,	7·69	69 6 11	
Woodcutting,	11·35	77 9 4	262 12 7
Total,	128·54		

CORK (MALE) PRISON—*continued.*

Return by the Governor, showing the employment of the Prisoners and value of their Earnings during the year ended 31st March, 1896.

Description of Employment.	Daily Average Number of Prisoners (for working days of the year).	Value of Prisoners' Labour.	Total.
In Buildings:—	M.	£ s. d.	£ s. d.
Bricklayers or masons,	·23	11 17 8	
Carpenters or joiners,	·78	5 16 0	
Labourers,	·29	6 1 6	
Painters and glaziers,	·74	19 10 8	
Plumbers and gasfitters,	·17	2 5 8	
Smiths,	·21	3 8 0	
Whitewashers,	·90	20 7 3	68 14 0
Total,	5·17		
In the ordinary service of the Prison:—			
Cleaning and jobbing work in and about the prison and prison yard and buildings (exclusive of building work of any kind),	25·19	435 0 0	
Cooking for the prisoners,	2·0	60 1 6	
Nursing and attending sick prisoners,	·85	33 8 4	
Pumping water for the service of the prison only,	4·59	82 2 0	
Repairing all kinds of prison clothing,	2·29	45 7 4	
Repairing all kinds of prison shoes,	1·00	30 4 8	
Repairing all kinds of prison utensils,	1·19	71 12 9	
Washing prisoners' clothing,	3·19	96 7 5	
Baking for prisoners,	2·0	52 0 0	976 15 9
Total,	47·15		
Non-effective:—			
Sick,	9·74	—	
Under punishment,	1·63	—	
Unemployed:—			
Awaiting trial,	3·19	—	
Debtors,	·19	—	
First class misdemeanants,	·41	—	
Others, &c.,	1·78	—	
Total,	16·72	—	
Grand Total,	156·16	—	1,[illegible] 15 6

CORK (FEMALE) PRISON.

Return by the Chief Warder, showing the employment of the Prisoners and value of their Earnings during the year ended 31st March, 1896.

Description of Employment.	Daily Average Number of Prisoners (for working days of the year).	Value of Prisoners' Labour.	Total.
In Manufactures:—	F.	£ s. d.	£ s. d.
Knitting and needleworking,	56·40	600 2 2	
Washing, not including prisoners' clothing,	1·0	7 1 1	607 3 3
Total,	57·40		
In Buildings:—			
Whitewashers,	·30	5 5 6	5 5 6
Total,	·30		

CORK (FEMALE) PRISON—*continued.*

RETURN by the CHIEF WARDER, showing the employment of the Prisoners and value of their Earnings during the year ended 31st March, 1896.

Description of Employment.	Daily Average Number of Prisoners (for working days of the year).	Value of Prisoners' Labour.	Total.
In the ordinary service of the Prison:—	F.	£ s. d.	£ s. d.
Cleaning and jobbing work in and about the prison and prison yard and buildings (exclusive of building work of any kind),	7·	187 11 4	
Cooking for the prisoners,	1·	89 [illegible] 8	
Nursing prisoners' children,	5·34	—	
Repairing all kinds of prison clothing,	·71	5 13 8	
Washing prisoners' clothing,	4·30	41 6 7	
Gardening,	·21	6 11 7	243 8 11
Total,	18·14		
Non-effective:—			
Sick,	6·	—	
Under punishment,	·25	—	
Unemployed:—			
Awaiting trial,	8·49	—	
Others, &c.,	4·	—	
Total,	18·74	—	
Grand Total,	[illegible]	—	1,[illegible] 18 10

DUNDALK (MALE) PRISON.

RETURN by the GOVERNOR, showing the employment of the Prisoners and value of their Earnings during the year ended 31st March, 1896.

Description of Employment.	Daily Average Number of Prisoners (for working days of the year).	Value of Prisoners' Labour.	Total.
In Manufactures:—	M.	£ s. d.	£ s. d.
Matmaking, plaiting, and other work connected therewith,	5·41	31 7 10	
Picking or teasing oakum, hair, &c., &c.,	3·71	4 13 0	
Stonebreaking,	11·65	5 13 6	
Woodcutting,	1·63	19 0 8	41 3 3
Total,	22·31		
In Buildings:—			
Carpenters or joiners,	·97	3 7 5	
Labourers,	1·20	25 1 7	
Painters and glaziers,	·24	9 8 11	
Whitewashers,	·25	6 6 1	44 19 5
Total,	2·1		
In the ordinary service of the Prison:—			
Cleaning and jobbing work in and about the prison and prison yard and buildings (exclusive of building work of any kind),	6·2	90 10 0	
Cooking for the prisoners,	1·94	48 7 11	
Pumping water for the service of the prison only,	3·62	80 9 11	
Repairing all kinds of prison clothing,	·19	14 17 1	
Repairing all kinds of prison shoes,	·76	14 6 2	
Washing prisoners' clothing,	1·7	57 8 11	
Gardening,	8·37	48 19 6	297 14 4
Total,	16·63		

DUNDALK (MALE) PRISON—*continued.*

RETURN by the GOVERNOR, showing the employment of the Prisoners and value of their Earnings during the year ended 31st March, 1896.

Description of Employment.	Daily Average Number of Prisoners (for working days of the year).	Value of Prisoners' Labour.	Total.
	M.	£ s. d.	£ s. d.
Non-effective:—			
Sick,	·25	—	
Under punishment,	·18	—	
Unemployed:—			
Awaiting trial,	1·71	—	
Debtors,	·22	—	
First class misdemeanants,	·01	—	
Others, &c.,	3·12	—	
Total,	5·06	—	
Grand Total,	46·04	—	293 11 7

GALWAY PRISON.

RETURN by the GOVERNOR, showing the employment of the Prisoners and value of their Earnings during the year ended 31st March, 1896.

Description of Employment.	Daily Average Number of Prisoners (for working days of the year).			Value of Prisoners' Labour.	Total.
	M.	F.	Total.	£ s. d.	£ s. d.
In Manufactures:—					
Mat-making, plaiting, and other work connected therewith,	1·48	—	1·48	6 6 9	
Picking or teasing oakum, hair, &c.,	5·14	—	5·14	—	
Stonebreaking,	16·71	—	16·71	51 9 1	
Washing, not including prisoners' clothing,	—	1·0	1·0	1 3 1	
Wood cutting,	2·48	—	2·48	17 1 3	
Carpet cleaning,	·22	—	·22	2 3 10	
Total,	25·83	1·0	27·03		100 0 3
In Buildings:—					
Bricklayers or masons,	·01	—	·01	0 6 0	
Carpenters or joiners,	·75	—	·75	7 10 6	
Labourers,	4·01	—	4·01	11 3 6	
Painters and glaziers,	·74	—	·74	14 11 5	
Smiths,	·12	—	·12	3 10 0	
Whitewashers,	1·07	·02	1·09	71 8 6	
Total,	6·70	·02	6·72		101 5 10
In the ordinary service of the Prison:—					
Cleaning and jobbing work in and about the prison and prison yard and buildings (exclusive of building work of any kind),	3·06	·07	3·13	67 17 6	
Cooking for the prisoners,	3·0	—	3·0	70 3 0	
Nursing and attending sick prisoners,	—	·93	·93	53 7 0	
Repairing all kinds of prison clothing,	·34	7·18	7·52	148 7 6	
Repairing all kinds of prison shoes,	·22	—	·22	0 3 3	
Washing prisoners' clothing,	—	2·03	2·03	36 6 0	
Gardening,	1·97	—	1·97	67 8 3	
Total,	7·61	10·98	17·97		374 13 6

GALWAY PRISON—*continued.*

RETURN by the GOVERNOR, showing the employment of the Prisoners and value of their Earnings during the year ended 31st March, 1896.

Description of Employment.	Daily Average Number of Prisoners (for working days of the year). M.	F.	Total.	Value of Prisoners' Labour. £ s. d.	Total. £ s. d.
Non-effective:—					
Sick,	·93	·79	1·72	—	
Under punishment,	·29	·09	·38	—	
Unemployed:—					
Awaiting trial,	6·33	·13	6·46	—	
Debtors,	·25	—	·25	—	
First class misdemeanants,	·61	·11	·76	—	
Others, &c.,	1·27	·73	1·57	—	
Total,	10·16	1·93	17·09	—	
Grand Total,	30·06	13·71	43·77	—	611 8 3

GRANGEGORMAN (FEMALE) PRISON.

RETURN by the SUPERINTENDENT, showing the employment of the Prisoners and value of their Earnings during the year ended 31st March, 1896.

Description of Employment.	Daily Average Number of Prisoners (for working days of the year). F.	Value of Prisoners' Labour. £ s. d.	Total. £ s. d.
In Manufactures:—			
Knitting and needleworking,	86·	1,542 18 0	
Picking or teasing oakum, hair, &c.,	6·50	0 9 1	
Washing, not including prisoners' clothing,	17·	221 5 0	1,[illegible] 12 1
Total,	108·50		
In Buildings:—			
Whitewashers,	1·	15 15 9	15 15 9
Total,	1·		
In the ordinary service of the Prison:—			
Cleaning and jobbing work in and about the prison and prison yard and buildings (exclusive of building work of any kind),	16·	265 0 0	
Repairing all kinds of prison clothing,	10·	139 7 0	
Washing prisoners' clothing,	11·	295 6 8	700 13 9
Total,	37·		
Non-effective:—			
Sick,	4·60	—	
Under punishment,	·30	—	
Unemployed:—			
Awaiting trial,	15·40	—	
Others, &c.,	6·78	—	
Total,	22·70	—	
Grand Total,	179·	—	2,210 4 7

KILKENNY (MALE) PRISON.

Return by the Governor, showing the employment of the Prisoners and value of their Earnings during the year ended 31st March, 1896.

Description of Employment.	Daily Average Number of Prisoners (for working days of the year).	Value of Prisoners' Labour.	Total.
In Manufactures :—	m.	£ s. d.	£ s. d.
Matmaking, plaiting, and other work connected therewith,	6·19	84 12 7	
Picking or teasing oakum, hair, &c.,	20·95	—	
Shoemaking,	3·48	190 1 10	
Stonebreaking,	4·63	84 19 4	
Tailoring,	·13	—	
Woodcutting,	7·21	25 9 6	
			286 15 9
Total,	43·77		
In Buildings :—			
Bricklayers or masons,	·18	3 16 9	
Carpenters or joiners,	·4	12 5 6	
Labourers,	1·34	31 6 7	
Painters and glaziers,	·43	11 6 9	
Smiths,	·04	1 4 7	
Whitewashers,	·3	7 11 8	
			67 11 4
Total,	6·06		
In the ordinary service of the Prison :—			
Cleaning and jobbing work in and about the prison and prison yard and buildings (exclusive of building work of any kind),	7·77	147 8 10	
Cooking for the prisoners,	6·	99 19 8	
Pumping water for the service of the prison only,	11·00	180 8 8	
Repairing all kinds of prison clothing,	6·10	78 15 7	
Repairing all kinds of prison shoes,	2·	97 11 8	
Stoking prison furnaces,	·3	19 17 6	
Washing prisoners' clothing,	5·62	72 9 9	
			487 17 1
Total,	31·46		
Non-effective :—			
Sick,	·87	—	
Under punishment,	·73	—	
Unemployed :—			
Awaiting trial,	1·21	—	
Debtors,	·15	—	
Exempt on payment for food,	·25	—	
First class misdemeanants,	·6	—	
Others, &c.,	6·18	—	
Total,	15·21	—	
Grand Total,	95·97	—	992 4 3

KILMAINHAM (MALE) PRISON.

RETURN by the GOVERNOR, showing the employment of the Prisoners and value of their Earnings during the year ended 31st March, 1898.

Description of Employment.	Daily Average Number of Prisoners (for working days of the year).	Value of Prisoners' Labour.	Total.
	m.	£ s. d.	£ s. d.
In Manufactures:—			
Picking or teasing oakum, hair, &c.,	11·29	0 17 6	
Sackmaking,	18·14	41 8 5	
Shoemaking,	7·19	68 1 3½	
Stonebreaking,	27·98	66 8 4	
Woodcutting,	8·79	29 7 8	
Do. for prison use,	1·	7 11 6	722 13 0¾
Total,	68·73		
In Buildings:—			
Bricklayers or masons,	·83	33 6 3½	
Carpenters or joiners,	·36	39 16 7¼	
Labourers,	3·76	36 16 8	
Painters and glaziers,	·36	27 16 0¾	
Plasterers,	·43	17 6 5¾	
Plumbers and Gasfitters,	·1	8 19 8	
Whitewashers,	·34	21 8 8½	178 1 9
Total,	5·86		
In the ordinary service of the Prison:—			
Cleaning and jobbing work in and about the prison and prison yards and buildings (exclusive of building work of any kind),	6·79	180 9 2½	
Cooking for the prisoners,	3·18	74 16 7¼	
Nursing and attending sick prisoners,	·3	16 8 7	
Repairing all kinds of prison clothing,	1·81	68 3 4½	
Repairing all kinds of prison shoes,	·77	18 7 4½	
Stoking prison furnaces,	1·	86 8 0	
Washing prisoners' clothing,	4·16	78 15 7	
Labourers,	7·46	180 7 8½	
Upholsterers,	·16	5 10 6¼	419 9 1½
Total,	27·27		
Non-effective:—			
Sick,	4·90	—	
Under punishment,	·37	—	
Unemployed:—			
Awaiting trial,	30·81	—	
Debtors,	·9	—	
Exempt on payment for food,	·13	—	
First class misdemeanants,	1·6	—	
Others, &c.,	1·13	—	
Total,	33·86	—	
Grand Total,	145·?4	—	1,0?? 6 7¼

LIMERICK (MALE) PRISON.

Return by the Governor, showing the employment of the Prisoners and value of their Earnings during the year ended 31st March, 1894.

Description of Employment.	Daily Average Number of Prisoners (for working days of the year.)	Value of Prisoners' Labour.	Total.
	No.	£ s. d.	£ s. d.
In Manufactures:—			
Mat-making, plaiting, and other work connected therewith,	5·4	15 10 3	
Picking or teasing oakum, hair, &c.,	7·47	—	
Shoemaking,	—	0 8 4	
Smithing and carpentry,	—	0 1 5	
Stonebreaking,	24·24	45 10 3	
Woodcutting,	0·84	[illegible] 17 1	
Total,	37·49		16[illegible] 17 5
In Buildings:—			
Bricklayers or masons,	·06	1 0 7	
Carpenters or joiners,	·64	12 17 7	
Painters and glaziers,	·24	31 5 8	
Whitewashers,	·7	4 1 6	
Total,	·95		[illegible] 7 5
In the ordinary service of the Prison:—			
Cleaning and jobbing work in and about the prison and prison yard and buildings (exclusive of building work of any kind),	10·84	704 0 5	
Cooking for the prisoners,	2·	45 1 5	
Nursing and attending sick prisoners,	·07	1 11 10	
Pumping water for the service of the prison only,	4·94	96 15 11	
Repairing all kinds of prison clothing,	1·74	87 10 0	
Repairing all kinds of prison shoes,	·65	36 1 11	
Total,	20·15		835 15 10
Non-effective:—			
Sick,	2·31	—	
Under punishment,	1·80	—	
Unemployed:—			
Awaiting trial,	11·55	—	
Debtors,	·35	—	
First-class misdemeanants,	·34	—	
Others, &c.,	7·00	—	
Total,	22·00	—	
Grand Total,	84·19	—	876 15 8

LIMERICK (FEMALE) PRISON.

RETURN by the CHIEF WARDER, showing the employment of the Prisoners and value of their Earnings during the year ended 31st March, 1896.

Description of Employment.	Daily Average Number of Prisoners (for working days of the year.)	Value of Prisoners' Labour.	Total.
	F.	£ s. d.	£ s. d.
In Manufactures;—			
Knitting and needleworking,	·18	0 5 4	
Washing, not including prisoners' clothing,	·44	—	0 5 4
Total,	·59		
In Buildings;—			
Painters and glaziers,	·16	4 18 5	
Whitewashers,	·33	5 14 9	10 13 2
Total,	·49		
In the ordinary service of the Prison;—			
Cleaning and jobbing work in and about the prison, and prison yard, and buildings (exclusive of building work of any kind),	6·85	95 12 6	
Cooking for the prisoners,	1·92	38 1 0	
Nursing children,	2·73	—	
Repairing all kinds of prison clothing,	21·91	467 10 8	
Washing prisoners' clothing,	3·76	71 4 1	650 8 11
Total,	34·71		
Non-effective;—			
Sick,	1·18	—	
Under punishment,	·71	—	
Unemployed;—			
Awaiting trial, &c.,	1·54	—	
Others, &c.,	6·86	—	
Total,	10·21	—	
Grand Total,	45·74	—	913 15 4

LONDONDERRY PRISON.

RETURN by the GOVERNOR, showing the employment of the Prisoners and value of their Earnings during the year ended 31st March, 1896.

Description of Employment.	Daily Average Number of Prisoners (for working days of the year.)			Value of Prisoners' Labour.	Total.
	M.	F.	Total.	£ s. d.	£ s. d.
In Manufactures;—					
Knitting and needleworking,	—	5·18	5·36	5 16 11	
Matmaking, Plaiting and other work connected therewith,	1·41	—	1·41	8 16 1	
Picking or teasing oakum, hair, &c.,	15·65	1·39	16·84	10 15 1	
Smithing,	·32	—	·15	2 14 8	
Stonebreaking,	6·93	—	6·93	3 17 8	
Washing, not including prisoners' clothing,	—	·78	·78	3 7 5	
Woodcutting,	4·73	—	5·74	25 9 9	
Carpet cleaning,	5·83	—	5·83	40 4 9	94 3 5
Total,	37·41	5·9	43·81		

LONDONDERRY PRISON—*continued.*

RETURN by the GOVERNOR, showing the employment of the Prisoners and value of their Earnings during the year ended 31st March, 1896.

Description of Employment.	Daily Average Number of Prisoners (for working days of the year.) M.	F.	Total.	Value of Prisoners' Labour. £ s. d.	Total. £ s. d.
In Buildings:—					
Bricklayers or masons,	·60	—	·60	9 0 9	
Carpenters or joiners,	·31	—	·31	7 0 9	
Labourers,	5·93	—	5·91	105 14 0	
Painters and glaziers,	·41	—	·41	0 1 8	
Whitewashers,	·41	—	·41	4 5 10	
Stonebreaking,	·25	—	·25	9 6 4	131 8 4
Total,	6·93	—	6·93		
In the ordinary service of the Prison:					
Cleaning and jobbing work in and about the prison and prison yard, and buildings (exclusive of building work of any kind),	7·53	1·76	9·29	104 4 7	
Cooking for the prisoners,	—	1·93	1·93	45 11 4	
Nursing and attending sick prisoners,	·85	·50	1·30	79 4 4	
Repairing all kinds of prison clothing,	1·14	13·76	14·9	284 19 9	
Repairing all kinds of prison shoes,	·46	—	·46	9 10 4	
Stoking prison furnaces,	·43	—	·43	4 10 8	
Washing prisoners' clothing,	—	5·19	5·19	54 8 8	
Gardening,	·15	—	·15	1 19 9	607 10 10
Total,	10·29	21·92	31·7		
Non-effective:—					
Sick,	2·37	·50	2·9	—	
Under punishment,	·04	·10	·14	—	
Unemployed:—					
Awaiting trial,	5·	1·39	6·19	—	
Debtors,	·37	·15	·50	—	
First class misdemeanants,	1·	—	1·	—	
Others, &c.,	6·15	1·25	7·47	—	
Total,	14·97	4·41	19·06	—	
Grand Total,	[illegible]	30·33	100·21	—	904 10 5

MOUNTJOY (MALE) PRISON.

RETURN by the GOVERNOR, showing the employment of the Prisoners and value of their Earnings during the year ended 31st March, 1896.

Description of Employment.	Daily Average Number of Prisoners (for working days of the year). M.	Value of Prisoners' Labour. £ s. d.	Total. £ s. d.
In Manufactures:—			
Brushmaking,	6·44	180 7 11	
Matmaking, plaiting, and other work connected therewith,	6·00	37 8 6	
Picking or teasing oakum, hair, &c.,	45·71	16 8 7	
Sackmaking,	25·19	110 1 1	
Shoemaking,	3·97	154 8 6	
Smithing (tin),	·77	8 4 8	
Stonebreaking,	5·	5 15 10	
Weaving frieze, &c.,	9·07	153 7 5	[illegible] 4 4
Total,	[illegible]		

MOUNTJOY (MALE) PRISON—*continued.*

RETURN by the GOVERNOR, showing the employment of the Prisoners and value of their Earnings during the year ended 31st March, 1896.

Description of Employment.	Daily Average Number of Prisoners (for working days of the year).	Value of Prisoners' Labour.	Total.
	M.	£ s. d.	£ s. d.
In Buildings:—			
Labourers,	7·23	[illegible] 6 1	
Painters and glaziers,	·73	66 11 [illegible]	
Stonebreaking,	18·97	57 14 [illegible]	
Whitewashers,	·75	16 14 [illegible]	
Total,	28·7[illegible]		[illegible] 1 [illegible]
In the ordinary service of the Prison:—			
Cleaning and jobbing work in and about the prison and prison yard and buildings (exclusive of building work of any kind),	12·01	277 10 [illegible]	
Cooking for the prisoners,	[illegible]	116 19 [illegible]	
Nursing and attending sick prisoners,	·39	10 [illegible] [illegible]	
Repairing all kinds of prison clothing,	[illegible]	175 [illegible] [illegible]	
Repairing all kinds of prison shoes,	1·[illegible]	19 10 1	
Total,	[illegible]		[illegible] 6 [illegible]
Non-effective:—			
Sick,	9·16	—	
Under punishment,	·[illegible]	—	
Unemployed:—			
Debtors,	·5	—	
Others, &c.,	35·31	—	
Total,	45·01	—	
Grand Total,	[illegible]	—	1,4[illegible] 6 [illegible]

SLIGO PRISON.

RETURN by the GOVERNOR, showing the employment of the Prisoners and value of their Earnings during the year ended 31st March, 1896.

Description of Employment.	Daily Average Number of Prisoners (for working days of the year).			Value of Prisoners' Labour.	Total.
	M.	F.	Total.	£ s. d.	£ s. d.
In Manufactures:—					
Knitting and needleworking,	—	[illegible]	[illegible]	0 [illegible] [illegible]	
Matmaking, plaiting, and other work connected therewith,	[illegible]	—	[illegible]	7 10 4	
Picking or teasing oakum, hair, &c.,	[illegible]	·21	[illegible]	—	
Stitching,	·12	—	·12	0 [illegible] [illegible]	
Stonebreaking,	13·[illegible]	—	13·[illegible]	[illegible] 16 [illegible]	
Washing, not including prisoners' clothing,	—	1·	1·	1 [illegible] 4	
Woodcutting,	[illegible]	—	[illegible]	[illegible] [illegible] 11	
Total,	[illegible]	[illegible]	[illegible]		[illegible] [illegible] [illegible]

SLIGO PRISON—*continued.*

RETURN by the GOVERNOR, showing the employment of the Prisoners and value of their Earnings during the year ended 31st March, 1896.

Description of Employment.	Daily Average Number of Prisoners (for working days of the year).			Value of Prisoners' Labour.	Total.
	M.	F.	Total.	£ s. d.	£ s. d.
In Buildings:—					
Carpenters or joiners,	·16	—	·16	6 19 7	
Painters and glaziers,	·16	—	·16	3 5 8	
Whitewashers,	·16	—	·16	4 18 10	
Total,	·48	—	·48		15 8 5
In the ordinary service of the Prison:—					
Cleaning and jobbing work in and about the prison and prison yard and buildings (exclusive of building work of any kind),	4·76	1·99	4·91	119 8 6	
Cooking for the prisoners,	1·	—	1·	89 0 0	
Nursing and attending sick prisoners,	—	1·82	1·82	41 7 8	
Prison garden,	·64	—	·64	19 3 4	
Repairing all kinds of prison clothing,	·46	5·	5·46	65 19 6	
Repairing all kinds of prison shoes,	·13	—	·13	5 6 5	
Washing prisoners' clothing,	—	1·61	1·61	20 9 9	
Total,	6·97	7·49	14·46		290 18 4
Non-effective:—					
Sick,	1·44	·46	1·90	—	
Under punishment,	·14	—	·14	—	
Unemployed:—					
Awaiting trial,	4·72	1·67	6·39	—	
Remanded on payment for food,	·06	—	·06	—	
First class misdemeanants,	1·21	2·98	6·20	—	
Others, &c.,	·96	·47	1·43	—	
Total,	6·98	4·80	11·26	—	
Grand Total,	40·45	17·12	57·57	—	344 5 5

TRALEE PRISON.

RETURN by the GOVERNOR, showing the employment of the Prisoners and value of their Earnings during the year ended 31st March, 1896.

Description of Employment.	Daily Average Number of Prisoners (for working days of the year).			Value of Prisoners' Labour.	Total.
	M.	F.	Total.	£ s. d.	£ s. d.
In Manufactures:—					
Carpentry,	·09	—	·09	0 1 9	
Picking or teasing oakum, hair, &c.,	5·26	—	5·26	—	
Stonebreaking,	10·11	—	10·11	71 15 9	
Tailoring,	·03	—	·03	0 1 3	
Washing, not including prisoners' clothing,	—	·40	·40	8 7 8	
Woodcutting,	3·02	—	3·02	3 9 4	
Total,	19·63	·40	20·03		85 14 8
In Buildings:—					
Bricklayers or masons,	·41	—	·41	14 8 8	
Carpenters or joiners,	·26	—	·26	8 11 9	
Labourers,	9·07	—	9·07	200 3 8	
Painters and glaziers,	·25	—	·25	11 5 9	
Whitewashers,	·25	—	·25	16 1 3	
Total,	11·06	—	11·06		240 11 11

TRALEE PRISON—*continued.*

RETURN by the GOVERNOR, showing the employment of the Prisoners and value of their Earnings during the year ended 31st March, 1898.

Description of Employment.	Daily Average Number of Prisoners (for working days of the year).			Value of Prisoners' Labour.	Total.
	M.	F.	Total.	£ s. d.	£ s. d.
In the ordinary service of the Prison :—					
Cleaning and jobbing work in and about the prison and prison yard and buildings (exclusive of building work of any kind),	7·17	—	7·17	39 3 5	
Cooking for the prisoners,	—	1·79	1·79	31 11 4	
Gardening,	7·70	—	7·70	40 7 6	
Nursing and attending sick prisoners,	—	·82	·82	6 10 9	
Repairing all kinds of prison clothing,	·07	[illegible]	8·76	64 1 5	
Repairing all kinds of prison shoes,	·39	—	·39	6 15 11	
Washing prisoners' clothing,	—	·43	·43	5 9 11	187 16 5
Total,	[illegible]	[illegible]	[illegible]		
Non-effective :—					
Sick,	·07	·01	·08	—	
Under punishment,	·24	·03	·27	—	
Unemployed :—					
Awaiting trial,	8·76	·18	8·94	—	
Debtors,	·21	—	·21	—	
First class misdemeanants,	·06	—	·06	—	
Others, &c.,	·61	·01	·07	—	
Total,	[illegible]	·23	5·22	—	
Grand Total,	41·24	[illegible]	[illegible]	—	437 9 10

TULLAMORE PRISON.

RETURN by the GOVERNOR, showing the employment of the Prisoners and value of their Earnings during the year ended 31st March, 1898.

Description of Employment.	Daily Average Number of Prisoners (for working days of the year).			Value of Prisoners' Labour.	Total.
	M.	F.	Total.	£ s. d.	£ s. d.
In Manufactures :—					
Knitting and needlework,	·33	·17	·45	1 7 9	
Picking or teasing oakum, hair, &c.,	7·66	·01	7·67	—	
Sackmaking,	34·72	—	34·72	69 19 5	
Shoemaking,	·36	—	·36	6 9 10	
Smithing,	·33	—	·33	6 5 4	
Stonebreaking,	·38	—	·38	1 7 9	
Washing, and mending prisoners' clothing,	—	9·69	9·69	5 5 1	
Woodcutting,	·65	—	·65	6 14 1	96 0 5
Total,	42·89	9·48	52·67		
In Buildings :—					
Carpenters or joiners,	·33	—	·33	8 15 0	
Labourers,	3·93	—	3·93	42 3 6	
Painters and glaziers,	·31	—	·31	7 15 9	
Whitewashers,	·33	—	·33	6 15 4	69 9 6
Total,	4·76	—	4·76		

TULLAMORE PRISON—*continued.*

RETURN by the GOVERNOR, showing the employment of the Prisoners and value of their Earnings during the year ended 31st March, 1896.

Description of Employment.	Daily Average Number of Prisoners (for working days of the year).			Value of Prisoners' Labour.	Total.
In the ordinary service of the Prison:—	M.	F.	Total.	£ s. d.	£ s. d.
Cleaning and jobbing work in and about the prison and prison yard and buildings (exclusive of building work of any kind),	6·37	·30	6·67	104 8 6	
Cooking for the prisoners,	3·	—	3·	45 1 6	
Nursing and attending sick prisoners,	·48	—	·48	16 11 6	
Pumping water for the service of the prison only,	2·39	—	2·39	45 5 6	
Repairing all kinds of prison clothing,	·80	9·94	10·74	158 6 6	
Repairing all kinds of prison shoes,	·81	—	·81	17 7 8	
Stoking prison furnaces,	·66	—	·66	10 8 6	
Washing prisoners' clothing,	—	8·40	8·40	57 7 6	
Total,	13·66	17·80	26·79		438 1 7
Non-effective:—					
Sick,	2·20	·15	2·37	—	
Under punishment,	·60	·05	·65	—	
Unemployed:—					
Awaiting trial,	4·32	1·03	5·35	—	
Debtors,	·61	—	·61	—	
First class misdemeanants,	·56	·00	·56	—	
Others, &c.,	3·34	1·96	5·30	—	
Total,	11·71	3·36	14·96	—	
Grand Total,	79·54	16·20	89·61	—	465 14 4

WATERFORD PRISON.

RETURN by the GOVERNOR, showing the employment of the Prisoners and value of their Earnings during the year ended 31st March, 1896.

Description of Employment.	Daily Average Number of Prisoners (for working days of the year).			Value of Prisoners' Labour.	Total.
Non-remunerative:	M.	F.	Total.	£ s. d.	£ s. d.
Picking rope junk,	4·66	—	4·66	—	—
In Manufactures:—					
Carpentering,	·30	—	·30	4 3 8	
Knitting and needleworking,	—	1·07	1·07	7 19 1	
Picking or teazing oakum, hair, &c.,	17·73	2·15	19·88	40 8 5	
Stonebreaking,	7·90	—	7·90	41 5 9	
Tailoring,	·01	—	·01	6 15 5	
Tin Smithing,	·01	—	·01	1 1 9	
Washing, not including prisoners' clothing,	—	1·40	1·40	46 11 9	
Woodcutting,	5·18	—	5·18	85 0 5	
Total,	83·10	4·66	87·76		278 6 6
In Buildings:—					
Bricklayers or masons,	·04	—	·04	1 17 6	
Carpenters or joiners,	·04	—	·04	3 10 9	
Painters and glaziers,	·22	—	·22	7 5 9	
Whitewashers,	·18	·04	·22	4 6 0	
Total,	·51	·04	·56		16 13 5

WATERFORD PRISON—*continued.*

RETURN by the GOVERNOR, showing the employment of the Prisoners and value of their Earnings during the year ended 31st March, 1896.

Description of Employment.	Daily Average Number of Prisoners (for working days of the year). M.	F.	Total	Value of Prisoners' Labour. £ s. d.	Total. £ s. d.
In the ordinary service of the Prison:—					
Cleaning and jobbing work in and about the prison and prison yard and buildings (exclusive of building work of any kind),	4·56	1·22	5·78	144 10 0	
Cooking for the prisoners,	—	1·91	1·91	46 10 0	
Nursing and attending sick prisoners,	—	1·77	1·77	39 0 0	
Pumping water for the service of the prison only,	1·99	—	1·99	10 15 0	
Repairing all kinds of prison clothing,	—	8·46	8·46	165 17 0	
Stoking prison furnaces,	·45	—	·45	11 11 0	
Washing prisoners' clothing,	·03	2·90	2·93	46 13 2	494 19 2
Total,	7·23	15·40	21·93		
Non-effective:—					
Sick,	·44	·26	·70	—	
Under punishment,	·10	·06	·16	—	
Unemployed:—					
Awaiting trial,	·78	·97	1·75	—	
Others,	·29	1·73	2·02	—	
Total,	1·[illegible]	[illegible]	4·21	—	
Grand Total,	[illegible]	21·17	[illegible]	—	[illegible] 0 7

WEXFORD PRISON.

RETURN by the GOVERNOR, showing the employment of the Prisoners and value of their Earnings during the year ended 31st March, 1896.

Description of Employment.	Daily Average Number of Prisoners (for working days of the year). M.	F.	Total	Value of Prisoners' Labour. £ s. d.	Total. £ s. d.
In Manufactures:—					
Mat-making, plaiting, and other work connected therewith,	9·16	—	9·16	10 8 2	
Picking or teasing oakum, hair, &c.	2·90	—	2·90	8 6 6	
Shoemaking,	·20	—	·20	0 4 4	
Stonebreaking,	1·75	—	1·75	9 12 0	
Tailoring,	·07	—	·07	0 0 0	
Washing, not including prisoners' clothing,	—	·08	·08	0 7 0	
Woodcutting,	0·32	—	0·32	0 10 0	14 18 6
Total,	10·18	·08	10·16		
In Buildings:—					
Painters and glaziers,	·40	—	·40	10 7 1	
Whitewashers,	·17	—	·17	0 7 0	13 14 7
Total,	·63	—	·63		

WEXFORD PRISON—*continued.*

RETURN by the GOVERNOR, showing the employment of the Prisoners and value of their Earnings during the year ended 31st March, 1896.

Description of Employment.	Daily Average Number of Prisoners (for working days of the year).			Value of Prisoners' Labour.	Total.
	M.	F.	Total	£ s. d.	£ s. d.
In the ordinary service of the Prison:—					
Cleaning and jobbing work in and about the prison and prison yard, and buildings (exclusive of building work of any kind),	2·96	1·78	4·24	50 0 0	
Cooking for the prisoners,	·85	·50	·99	8 16 7	
Pumping water for the service of the prison only,	·25	—	·25	4 0 0	
Repairing all kinds of prison clothing,	·16	2·35	2·45	81 4 4	
Washing prisoners' clothing,	·60	—	·60	16 9 6	
Total,	4·95	3·60	7·71		161 0 6
Non-effective:—					
Sick,	·20	·01	·25	—	
Under punishment,	·16	—	·10	—	
Unemployed:—					
Awaiting trial,	2·15	·33	2·48	—	
Debtors,	·19	—	·19	—	
First class misdemeanants,	·82	·16	1·06	—	
Others, &c.	1·04	·42	1·90	—	
Total,	4·19	·83	5·61	—	
Grand Total,	24·29	4·64	29·17	—	[illegible] 18 4

MINOR PRISONS.

CARRICK-ON-SHANNON PRISON.

RETURN by the CHIEF WARDER, showing the employment of the Prisoners and value of their Earnings during the year ended 31st March, 1896.

Description of Employment.	Daily Average Number of Prisoners (for working days of the year).			Value of Prisoners' Labour.	Total.
	M.	F.	Total	£ s. d.	£ s. d.
Non-remunerative:—					
Picking oakum,	·27	—	·27	—	
In Buildings:—					
Whitewashers,	·10	—	·10	4 16 3	4 16 3
In the ordinary service of the Prison:—					
Cleaning and jobbing work in and about the prison and prison yard, and buildings (exclusive of building work of any kind),	·43	·10	·43	13 7 3	
Repairing all kinds of prison clothing,	—	·04	·04	1 0 0	
Washing prisoners' clothing,	—	·13	·13	0 10 0	
Total,	·53	·23	·84		15 17 3
Unemployed:—					
Awaiting trial,	1·26	·2	1·24	—	
Total,	1·30	·0	1·33	—	
Grand Total,	2·23	·40	2·73	—	20 14 2

DROGHEDA PRISON.

RETURN by the CHIEF WARDER, showing the employment of the Prisoners and value of their Earnings during the year ended 31st March, 1896.

Description of Employment.	Daily Average Number of Prisoners (for working days of the year).			Value of Prisoners' Labour.	Total.
	M.	F.	Total.	£ s. d.	£ s. d.
In Manufactures :—					
Knitting and needleworking,	—	·01	·01	0 5 0	
Picking or teasing oakum, hair, &c.,	1·[illegible]	—	1·0[illegible]	0 7 0	
Stonebreaking,	·01	—	·01	0 3 0	
Woodcutting,	·[illegible]	—	·[illegible]	3 10 6	
Total,	1·34	·01	1·35		4 5 6
In Buildings :—					
Painters and glaziers,	·01	—	·01	0 10 0	
Whitewashers,	·12	—	·12	3 8 9	
Total,	·13	—	·13		3 18 9
In the ordinary service of the Prison :—					
Cleaning and jobbing work in and about the prison and prison yard, and buildings (exclusive of building work of any kind),	·71	·12	·83	15 11 0	
Cooking for the prisoners,	·[illegible]	·01	·71	22 11 0	
Nursing and attending children,	—	·24	·24	—	
Repairing all kinds of prison clothing,	—	·66	·66	0 10 6	
Washing prisoners' clothing,	—	·70	·70	1 16 5	
Total,	1·[illegible]	1·16	2·17		44 [illegible] 0
Non-effective :—					
Sick,	·[illegible]	·01	·[illegible]	—	
Unemployed :—					
Awaiting trial,	·[illegible]	·[illegible]	1·26	—	
Total,	·[illegible]	·31	1·2[illegible]	—	
Grand Total,	[illegible]	1·4[illegible]	[illegible]	—	51 19 3

ENNISKILLEN PRISON.

RETURN by the CHIEF WARDER, showing the employment of the Prisoners and value of their Earnings, during the year ended 31st March, 1896.

Description of Employment.	Daily Average Number of Prisoners (for working days of the year).			Value of Prisoners' Labour.	Total.
	M.	F.	Total.	£ s. d.	£ s. d.
Non-Remunerative,	·04	·04	·08	—	
In Manufactures :—					
Stonebreaking,	·11	—	·11	1 3 0	
Woodcutting,	·12	—	·12	0 6 9	
Total,	·23	—	·23		1 10 0
In Buildings :—					
Painters and glaziers,	·04	—	·04	0 14 1	
Whitewashers,	·16	—	·16	2 15 1	
Total,	·20	—	·20		3 9 2

ENNISKILLEN PRISON—*continued.*

RETURN by the CHIEF WARDER, showing the employment of the Prisoners and value of their Earnings during the year ended 31st March, 1898.

Description of Employment.	Daily Average Number of Prisoners (for working days of the year).			Value of Prisoners' Labour.	Total.
	M.	F.	Total	£ s. d.	£ s. d.
In the ordinary service of the Prison:—					
Cleaning and jobbing work in and about the prison and prison yard, and buildings (exclusive of building work of any kind),	·35	·11	·46	4 0 10½	
Gardening,	·21	—	·21	1 0 7½	
Repairing all kinds of prison clothing,	·23	·08	·31	1 0 0	
Washing prisoners' clothing,	·05	·14	·19	1 10 0	8 2 6
Total,	·84	·33	1·17		
Non-effective:—					
Sick,	·03	·02	·05	—	
Under punishment,	·03	·01	·03	—	
Unemployed:					
Awaiting trial,	·58	·18	·76	—	
Total,	·64	·28	·94	—	
Grand Total,	1·57	·61	2·23	—	10 1 6

MULLINGAR PRISON.

RETURN by the CHIEF WARDER, showing the employment of the Prisoners and value of their Earnings during the year ended 31st March, 1898.

Description of Employment.	Daily Average Number of Prisoners (for working days of the year).			Value of Prisoners' Labour.	Total.
	M.	F.	Total	£ s. d.	£ s. d.
In Manufactures:—					
Picking or teasing oakum, hair, &c.,	·79	·42	1·21	—	
Stonebreaking,	1·13	—	1·13	1 6 0	
Woodcutting,	·07	—	·07	0 6 6	1 11 6
Total,	1·99	·42	2·41		
In Buildings:—					
Labourers,	·67	—	·67	14 10 0	
Painters and glaziers,	·28	—	·28	5 5 5	
Whitewashers,	·27	—	·27	5 16 6	25 [illegible] 11
Total,	1·22	—	1·22		
In the ordinary service of the Prison:—					
Cleaning and jobbing work in and about the prison and prison yard, and buildings (exclusive of building work of any kind),	·91	·34	1·25	18 15 0	
Pumping water for the service of the prison only,	·05	—	·05	1 12 3	
Repairing all kinds of prison clothing,	—	·11	·11	2 1 6	
Washing prisoners' clothing,	—	·76	·76	14 7 10	37 0 0
Total,	·96	1·21	2·17		
Non-effective:—					
Sick,	·07	·21	·28	—	
Under punishment,	·04	—	·04	—	
Unemployed:—					
Awaiting trial,	·08	·02	·10	—	
Total,	·19	·23	·42	—	
Grand Total,	4·36	1·86	6·22	—	67 18 1

OMAGH PRISON.

Return by the Chief Warder, showing the employment of the Prisoners and value of their Earnings during the year ended 31st March, 1896.

Description of Employment.	Daily Average Number of Prisoners (for working days of the year).			Value of Prisoners' Labour.	Total.
	M.	F.	Total.	£ s. d.	£ s. d.
Non-Remunerative:—					
Picking and teasing oakum,	·21	·1	·31	—	
In Manufactures:—					
Stonebreaking,	·56	—	·56	1 16 11	
Woodcutting,	·9	—	·9	4 11 0	
Total,	1·46	—	1·46		6 7 11
In Buildings:—					
Bricklayers or masons,	·01	—	·01	0 10 9	
Carpenters or joiners,	·08	—	·08	0 9 5	
Labourers,	·18	—	·18	2 14 4	
Painters and glaziers,	·12	—	·12	4 19 7	
Plasterers,	·03	—	·03	1 7 8	
Smiths,	·02	—	·02	1 4 0	
Whitewashers,	·11	—	·11	7 14 4	
Total,	·55	—	·55		18 15 10
In the ordinary service of the Prison:—					
Cleaning and jobbing work in and about the prison and prison yard, and buildings (exclusive of building work of any kind),	·67	·04	·71	13 12 9	
Nursing and attending sick prisoners,	·02	·03	·05	6 12 0	
Repairing all kinds of prison clothing,	·11	·04	·15	9 10 0	
Washing prisoners' clothing,	—	·18	·18	5 5 9	
Total,	·80	·29	1·1		32 10 5
Non-effective:—					
Sick,	·02	—	·02	—	
Under punishment,	·03	—	·03	—	
Unemployed:—					
Awaiting trial,	1·05	·11	1·16	—	
Debtors,	·1	·03	·13	—	
First class misdemeanants,	·04	—	·04	—	
Others, &c.,	·09	·08	·17	—	
Total,	1·23	·2	1·43	—	
Grand Total,	4·19	·58	4·77	—	63 14 8

WICKLOW PRISON.

Return by the Chief Warder, showing the employment of the Prisoners and value of their Earnings during the year ended 31st March, 1896.

Description of Employment.	Daily Average Number of Prisoners (for working days of the year).			Value of Prisoners' Labour.	Total.
	M.	F.	Total.	£ s. d.	£ s. d.
In Manufactures:—					
Picking or teasing oakum, hair, &c.,	·63	—	·63	6 6 7	6 6 7
Total	·63	—	·63		

WICKLOW PRISON—*continued.*

Return by the Chief Warder, showing the employment of the Prisoners and value of their Earnings during the year ended 31st March, 1896.

Description of Employment.	Daily Average Number of Prisoners (for working days of the year).			Value of Prisoners' Labour.	Total.
	M.	F.	Total.	£ s. d.	£ s. d.
In Buildings:—					
Painters and glaziers,	·03	—	·03	0 10 8	
Whitewashers,	·10	—	·10	2 10 4	
Total,	·13	—	·13		3 10 9
In the ordinary service of the Prison:—					
Cleaning and jobbing work in and about the prison and prison yard, and buildings (exclusive of building work of any kind),	·74	·08	·82	15 14 4	
Cooking for the prisoners,	·09	—	·09	2 12 5	
Pumping water for the service of the prison only,	·44	—	·44	8 14 8	
Repairing all kinds of prison clothing,	—	·08	·08	1 10 4	
Washing prisoners' clothing,	—	·09	·09	2 11 1	
Woodcutting,	·12	—	·12	0 10 8	
Total,	1·41	[illegible]	1·67		31 8 5
Non-effective:—					
Sick,	·01	·01	·02	—	
Under punishment,	·01	—	·01	—	
Unemployed:—					
Awaiting trial,	1·72	·14	1·87	—	
Total,	1·73	·15	1·90	—	
Grand Total,	[illegible]	·41	[illegible]	—	34 14 9

APPENDIX

PART III

CONVICT PRISONS.

REPORTS AND TABLES.

Mary-borough Male Convict Prison.

Governor's Report.

MARYBOROUGH CONVICT PRISON

(For Invalid and Intermediate Class Convicts, and other selected Convicts).

GOVERNOR'S REPORT.

H. M. Convict Prison, Maryborough,
May 5th, 1896.

Sir,—I have the honour to submit my report on the condition of this prison during the year ended 31st March, 1896, as required by Rule "185." The statistical returns for the calendar year have been forwarded to Board's Office on 10th February in compliance with instructions contained in circular letters, dated 31st October and 23rd December, 1895, as distinguished from the financial year, the period for which such statistics had previously been rendered, and to which my report refers.

The conduct of the subordinate officers has been very satisfactory generally. Only in one instance has there occurred amongst them a case of such serious dereliction of duty as to involve fine by Board. The Chief Warder has given efficient and valuable assistance in maintaining discipline amongst officers and prisoners. One officer was discharged on superannuation, one transferred to Wexford prison on promotion, three were received from Mountjoy, and one from Kilmainham. The staff has been thus increased by two warders, that those for evening duties might be relieved off duty for an equivalent of time during the day. This valuable privilege has been duly appreciated.

There were 67 convicts in custody on 1st January, 1895:—received during the year, 41; discharged, 47; removed to Dundrum Asylum, 2; died, 1; remaining in custody 31st December, 58. There were in Intermediate class, 5. Received during year, 25; discharged on licence, 19; remaining in class, 11.

These have been employed outside the prison, as far as circumstances would permit, cultivating the land, by which a sufficient supply of vegetables for the use of the prison for the whole year has been produced. Vegetables have also been sold to the warders and their families.

About 100 square perches of potatoes were grown. With sanction of Board I purchased a knapsack sprayer, and with a solution of sulphate of copper and lime I had them treated about end of July with very satisfactory results—those treated having continued to grow, when those which had not been sprayed had been quite decayed. The produce was largely increased, and the tubers were not affected by blight. The quantity of potatoes grown on this comparatively small space represented a saving to the public of £38 10s.

The two new cottages which had just been commenced in January, 1895, have been finished, one of them being occupied on 1st February, and the other on 1st April this year, thus affording much needed accommodation for the number of married officers at present on the staff-book—viz., 12—and saving the expenditure on lodging allowance.

The necessary repairs to the prison buildings have been regularly attended to.

The conduct of the prisoners in the Intermediate Class has been most satisfactory. Previous to their discharge I have communicated with the clergyman of the districts in which they were respectively about to reside, stating that the General Prisons Board took a great interest in their welfare, and requesting that everything suitable and convenient might be done in furtherance of their desire to obtain employment, and the means of earning a livelihood by honesty and industry. I have in some instances received favourable replies.

MARYBOROUGH MALE CONVICT PRISON. — *Governor's Report.*

The invalid prisoners when not seriously ill, and when "fit for work" have been suitably employed at shoemaking, tailoring, cooking, cleaning prison, and tilling the garden inside the prison walls. Their conduct generally has been very good, the cases of misconduct being few in number and slight in character. In only one case was it found necessary to use restraint for a few hours on a prisoner as a preventive against violence. He was afterwards removed to Dundrum Asylum.

The prisoners of the invalid class are all under special medical treatment for specific diseases, yet their health has been well maintained, and only one death occurred during the year.

There have been no escapes, attempts to escape, or suicides during the year.

The late Resident Medical Officer, Dr. O'Connell, was retired on superannuation after forty years service, his office having been filled by Dr. Kinsella, who had served in Mountjoy for some years—a zealous, attentive, and deserving officer, under whose care, and that of the eminent Consulting Visiting Physician, the health of the prisoners has received unremitting attention.

The Chaplains have been zealous and attentive, willingly co-operating in any effort for the improvement and reformation of the prisoners whilst in prison, and also in endeavouring to obtain employment for them after their discharge.

The morning and evening schools have been conducted as in former years with very satisfactory results, the progress made by some of the prisoners being much greater than could reasonably have been expected, having regard to their age and opportunities. The library has been fully availed of, and the books provided annually are much appreciated.

A farm of thirty-four acres has just been purchased, possession of which was received on 31st March.

Draining and reclaiming this land, bringing it into a state of productive cultivation, will afford abundant employment for some years, and of a kind which should be beneficial to many of the convicts after their discharge, as rendering them more suitable for the occupation of farmers or farm labourers.

The season was so far advanced when possession was taken, that little cultivation can be done on the land this year, but the necessary preparations are being made for enclosing it with a wall on which work will be commenced immediately.

I certify that the Rules laid down for the government of the prison have been complied with to the best of my knowledge and belief, except in such cases as have been specially reported to the Board.

I take the liberty to gratefully acknowledge the valuable advice and assistance given by the Visiting Committee who visited the prison on 10th April, 8th May, 12th June, 10th July, 14th August, 11th September, 9th October, 13th November, 11th December, 1895; and on 15th January, 12th February, and 11th March, 1896.

I have the honour to be, Sir,

Your obedient servant,

JOHN CONDON, Governor.

To Chairman,
General Prisons Board,
Dublin Castle.

MARYBOROUGH MALE CONVICT PRISON.

Protestant Episcopalian Chaplain's Report.

PROTESTANT EPISCOPALIAN CHAPLAIN'S REPORT.

The Rectory, Maryborough,

22nd April, 1896.

SIR,—The prisoners were during the past year as usual very quiet and attentive while attending the services in connexion with the Church of Ireland. As far as I was able to learn from visiting them in their cells they were generally orderly in their behaviour, and with few exceptions expressed themselves satisfied with the treatment they were receiving. I find the experience of a Prison Chaplain varies but little from year to year; a few openly avow that they have no regard for religion, but most appear penitent and anxious to reform. It is disappointing to find so many relapse into criminal habits on obtaining their freedom. The moral faculty, whether by nature or habit, is weak, and prudential considerations are ineffectual to produce the desired change. This is, I believe, the reason more marked results do not follow from all that is done for them.

I have the honour to be, Sir,

Your obedient servant,

EDMD. L. EYRE.

P.S.—I have reason to believe that the prisoners made fair progress in the school, some of them spoke to me of the advantage it was to them.

The Chairman, General Prisons Board.

Roman Catholic Chaplain's Report.

ROMAN CATHOLIC CHAPLAIN'S REPORT.

Maryboro',

13th April, 1896.

GENTLEMEN,—I have not many remarks to make about our prison here during the past year. Taking into account the infirmities, mental and physical, of the prisoners, I think their conduct has been satisfactory. They appear to take a great interest in the school duties, and in reading the books provided for them in the library.

I am glad that the Prison Authorities have acquired additional land adjoining the prison, as the work in it will relieve the monotony of the prison life, and will be a healthy exercise for the prisoners. The Governor and other officials afford every facility and assistance to the Chaplains in the discharge of their duties.

I remain, Gentlemen, yours faithfully,

A. PHELAN, P.P.

To the Chairman of Prisons Board.

MARY-BOROUGH MALE CONVICT PRISON.

MEDICAL OFFICERS' REPORT.

H. M. Convict Prison, Maryboro',

6th May, 1896.

Medical Officers' Report.

We have the honour to submit the annual report on the health of the officers and prisoners under our care, and the sanitary condition of the prison for the year ending the 31st March, 1896.

The number of convicts admitted to hospital during the year was 14 (fourteen), and we have to record but one death, which was caused by apoplexy.

The number of extern cases for the year amounted to 594, mostly for trivial and passing ailments.

During the same period three prisoners were certified insane, and transferred to Dundrum Criminal Lunatic Asylum. From the invalid class 4 (four) were released on medical grounds.

Subordinate officers off duty during the year by illness numbered 12 (twelve), all for short periods and slight ailments. No death occurred amongst the staff. One warder, found to be physically unfit for duty, was retired on pension.

As to the families of the staff nothing special calls for remark. The water supply to the prison is abundant and good, and the sanitary condition of the several buildings apparently most satisfactory.

In conclusion, we have very great pleasure in acknowledging the facilities and support in the performance of our duties afforded to us by the Governor and the staff under his guidance.

J. I. KINSELLA,

Physician, Surgeon, and L.M.

D. B. JACOB, M.D.,

Consulting and Visiting Physician.

MOUNTJOY CONVICT PRISON.

MOUNTJOY CONVICT PRISON.

GOVERNOR'S REPORT.

Governor's Report.

Mountjoy Prison,

April, 1896.

SIR,—I have the honour to report for the year ended 31st March, 1896, on the Mountjoy Convict Prison as follows:—

The subordinate officers have been generally well conducted, attentive to their duties, and careful in the discharge of them. None were dismissed or reduced in rank during the year. The Chief and Principal Warders have discharged their duties with zeal and efficiency.

The reduction in the hours of duty of the subordinate officers, which was ordered by the Board, has been a great boon, and is highly appreciated by the staff.

The convicts have, with some few exceptions, been generally well-behaved, and they have usually performed the work allotted to them with diligence, and many with taste and skill. Punishments for prison offences or for deliberate breaches of rule have been comparatively few, when the training, dispositions, and antecedents of many confined have been taken into account; nevertheless good order and strict discipline have been well-maintained.

Mountjoy Convict Prison. — Governor's Report.

There was no case of corporal punishment during the year.

There was no escape or attempt to escape, although convicts were constantly employed outside the prison walls, and often in unsafe places; this tells well for the vigilance of the officers.

The employments of the convicts during the year have been generally the same as detailed in former reports.

I expect to have twenty-three new houses outside the prison walls, which have been entirely built by convict labour, ready for the occupation of the subordinate officers by the 1st May. There will then be sixty houses (fifty of which have been built during the last few years by convict labour) close to the prison, and the property of the General Prisons Board, occupied by the subordinate married officers of the convict and local prisons and their families, where they are more comfortably circumstanced, and have much better accommodation than they could possibly obtain elsewhere near the prison, for the amount sanctioned as lodging allowance.

The buildings both within and outside the prison walls, which are the property of the General Prisons Board, have been kept in proper repair and in good order by convict labour.

The chaplains have been regular in their attendances, and have taken much interest in the temporal, as well as the spiritual, welfare of the convicts committed to their care. The Protestant and both the Roman Catholic Chaplains are active members of prisoners' aid societies.

The schooling continues same as in previous years, and the teachers have been attentive and diligent.

I certify that the rules laid down for the government of the prison have been adhered to, except in such cases as have been brought to the notice of the General Prisons Board.

I have the honour to be, Sir,

Your most obedient servant,

Geo. Sheehan, Governor.

The Chairman, General Prisons Board.

Protestant Episcopalian Chaplain's Report.

PROTESTANT EPISCOPALIAN CHAPLAIN'S REPORT.

H. M. Prison, Mountjoy, Dublin,

April 24, 1896.

Sir,—In submitting my Annual Report I have pleasure in stating that in the department of which I have charge everything, I may say, has gone on satisfactorily. The Church Services have been held regularly throughout the year without a single exception. The demeanour of the prisoners during Divine Worship has been most excellent. They take the share allotted to them in our Liturgy, and are very attentive during the sermon on Sundays, and during religious instruction on week-days.

I advise those of the convicts—more especially the younger men—who may be backward in their education, to be diligent and industrious in the prison school. I find, on enquiry, that in many of these cases satisfactory progress has been made during the twelve months. I consider this a matter of congratulation for all concerned, and a superior advantage to the convicts themselves on discharge from gaol.

During the year I had but one case of serious illness where the malady, though the patient was advanced in life, did not prove fatal. I have had a lengthened experience of attendance at sick beds, and I cannot recall to my mind a greater instance of medical skill, which was materially supplemented by careful nursing, as well as by the fine commodious infirmary of the prison.

Mountjoy Convict Prison. — *Protestant Episcopalian Chaplain's Report.*

I beg to thank the excellent Governor, George S. Sheahan, Esq.—at all times unremitting in his exertions—and the rest of his working staff for kind co-operation.

I have the honour, Sir, to remain

Your obedient servant,

JOHN H. MACMAHON, M.A., LL.D.,

Protestant Chaplain.

To the Chairman of the General Prisons Board.

ROMAN CATHOLIC CHAPLAINS' REPORT.

Roman Catholic Chaplains' Report.

Mountjoy Prison, June, 1896.

SIR,—It affords us much pleasure, in presenting our annual Report, to bear testimony to the satisfactory condition of the prisoners committed to our spiritual charge. They were, we are happy to say, all that could well be expected. We found them, as a body, attentive to our religious instructions, and the great majority of them received the Sacraments of the Church frequently and devoutly.

In our intercourse with them in the different parts of the Prison we found them cheerful and docile, and ready to carry out any suggestion we should deem it advisable to make to them.

The general discipline of the Prison was, we are of opinion, very good. There were, comparatively, few breaches of rule, and those not of a very serious nature.

We beg to tender to the Governor, to the Medical Officers, and to the other prison officials, our sincere thanks for the kindness and courtesy we received from them in the discharge of our duties.

We have the honour to be, Sir, your humble servants,

M. WALSH, R.C.C.

T. O'DONNELL, Asst. R.C.C.

PRESBYTERIAN CHAPLAIN'S REPORT.

Presbyterian Chaplain's Report.

Mountjoy Convict Prison,

April 16, 1896.

The year ending March 31st, 1896, has been a peculiarly uneventful one in the life and work of the prison as far as my department is concerned. The prisoners under my care have been very attentive to instruction, and when I have thought it my duty to counsel them, they have accepted my advice gratefully. Their good conduct marks show a very creditable record for the year. I have endeavoured, as far as possible, to keep track of the prisoners under my care after they have

Mountjoy Convict Prison. — Presbyterian Chaplain's Report.

been discharged from prison. It is a pleasure to find some of them thoroughly recovering their character, and proving useful citizens. I may add, the number of Presbyterian convict prisoners, which is very small in proportion to the Presbyterian population, seems to be growing steadily less.

I have the honour to be, Gentleman,

Your obedient servant,

J. C. Johnston,

Presbyterian Chaplain.

H. M.'s General Prisons Board.

Medical Officer's Report.

MEDICAL OFFICER'S REPORT.

Mountjoy Convict Prison,

26th February, 1896.

SIR,—I have the honour to submit the annual report on the sanitary state of this prison, with the usual medical statistics, for the year ended 31st December last.

During the year there were 37 warders admitted into hospital. The chief ailments were:—Influenza, bronchitis, febricula, rheumatism, and catarrh. No death or other serious casualty occurred.

On the 1st January, 1895, there remained in hospital 20 convicts, and during the year 251 others were admitted, chiefly for influenza, bronchitis, febricula, debility, rheumatism, and dyspepsia. Of those treated in hospital 234 were discharged to their classes, 10 were transferred to the invalid prison, 4 were removed to the Criminal Lunatic Asylum, 3 were discharged from prison on medical grounds. There were 3 deaths, and 17 remained in hospital on the 31st December.

Influenza was prevalent during the months of March and April; the other diseases were such as occur in ordinary life.

During the year the health of the officers and the prisoners was generally good, and strict attention was paid to the sanitary arrangements of the prison.

I have the honour to be, Sir,

Your obedient servant,

P. O'Keeffe, M.D.,

Medical Officer.

The Chairman, General Prisons Board,
Dublin Castle.

Grangegorman Female Convict Prison. — Superintendent's Report.

GRANGEGORMAN FEMALE CONVICT PRISON.

SUPERINTENDENT'S REPORT.

H. M. Prison, Grangegorman,

2nd May, 1896.

SIR,—I have the honour to submit my annual report on the convict portion of Grangegorman Prison, with statistical returns.

The subordinate officers have been well conducted and attentive to their duties during the year.

The convicts have been exceedingly well conducted and industrious. They are principally employed in laundry work, knitting and sewing, whitewashing and painting. Three have been constantly employed in the kitchen, cooking for convict and local prisoners.

GRANGE-GORMAN FEMALE CONVICT PRISON. — *Superintendent's Report.*

The school has been satisfactorily worked, the teacher being zealous and painstaking.

The Sisters of Charity still continue to visit and instruct the Roman Catholic prisoners, while a Protestant lady visitor visits and instructs the Protestant prisoners.

I certify that the rules laid down for the government of the prison have been adhered to, except in such cases as have been brought to the notice of the Prisons Board.

I have the honour to be, Sir,

Your obedient servant,

CATHERINE J. M'CARTHY,
Superintendent.

The Chairman, General Prisons Board,
Dublin Castle.

PROTESTANT EPISCOPALIAN CHAPLAIN'S REPORT.

Protestant Episcopalian Chaplain's Report.

H. M. Prison, Grangegorman,
May, 1896.

SIR,—In furnishing my annual report of Grangegorman Convict Prison I have little to add to former reports.

The number of Church of Ireland Protestant convicts in prison on March 31, 1896, was four. Of these two are intelligent and remarkably well instructed, but belong to a class very difficult to influence for good; a third is a repeatedly-returned convict, very ignorant, and too old to learn; another, quite illiterate, has made some progress in learning to read, and is anxious to profit by the instruction given.

In my opinion the discipline of the prison is good, and the officers efficient and considerate to the prisoners.

I remain yours faithfully,

HENRY HOGAN.

To the Chairman of the
General Prisons Board.

ROMAN CATHOLIC CHAPLAIN'S REPORT.

Roman Catholic Chaplain's Report.

Grangegorman Prison,

May 4th, 1896.

SIR,—I have the honour to submit my Report for the year ended March 31st.

The Roman Catholic prisoners, without a single exception, attended their religious duties during the past year, and their conduct was better than I have known it to be since the convicts were sent here in 1883.

Discipline was enforced and good order maintained without any harsh treatment of the prisoners, a fact which reflects the highest credit on the officers in charge.

Grangegorman Female Convict Prison. — Roman Catholic Chaplain's Report.

Now, that so many changes in Prison Rules, Classification, &c., have been suggested to Government, may I be permitted to state what I believe would reduce the Irish Female Prison population to the lowest possible figure. An establishment should be opened for the detention of habitual offenders, and should be conducted on substantially the same lines as the Reformatory Schools for juvenile offenders. The sentence should be for a term not shorter than five years, and the Superintendent should have the same powers as the Managers of Reformatories. To all objections that might be raised, I should answer that this plan is, as a matter of fact, the one that was adopted for years with the female convicts in Golden Bridge Refuge, with the result that 90 per cent. were reformed, as may be seen from the evidence submitted to the Royal Commission on Irish Prisons of 1883.

I know that many excellent people are opposed, from motives of humanity, to long sentences for women, but I suspect these good people have not had an opportunity of making themselves thoroughly acquainted with the almost incredible success attained by the system at Golden Bridge.

I have the honour to be, Sir,

Your obedient servant,

James Anderson.

Presbyterian Chaplain's Report.

PRESBYTERIAN CHAPLAIN'S REPORT.

Grangegorman Prison,

21/4/96.

Gentlemen,—There is only one Presbyterian convict prisoner under my care. She was sentenced to a term of three years five months ago. She had been discharged but a very short time from a lunatic asylum when convicted as "not improved."

I have the honour to be, Gentlemen,

Your obedient servant,

J. C. Johnston.

H. M.'s General Prisons Board.

Medical Officer's Report.

MEDICAL OFFICER'S REPORT.

H. M. Prison, Grangegorman,

9th May, 1896.

Sir,—In submitting the usual Annual Report for the year ended 31st March, 1896, I beg to state that the general health, both of officers and prisoners has been good, and that no death has occurred during this period.

The sanitary state of the Prison is effectively maintained.

I have the honour to be, Sir,

TABLE XXI. Number of [illegible] under [illegible], and Disposal of same, &c., during the Year ended 31st December, [illegible].

[illegible]	[illegible]	[illegible]	[illegible]	[illegible]	[illegible]	[illegible]	[illegible]
[illegible]	[illegible]	[illegible]	[illegible]	[illegible]	[illegible]	[illegible]	[illegible]
Total,	[illegible]	[illegible]	[illegible]	[illegible]	[illegible]	[illegible]	[illegible]
[illegible]	[illegible]	[illegible]	[illegible]	[illegible]	[illegible]	[illegible]	[illegible]
Total disposed of during the year,	[illegible]	[illegible]	[illegible]	[illegible]	[illegible]	[illegible]	[illegible]
„ remaining in custody at end of year,	[illegible]	[illegible]	[illegible]	[illegible]	[illegible]	[illegible]	[illegible]
Total,	[illegible]	[illegible]	[illegible]	[illegible]	[illegible]	[illegible]	[illegible]
Daily average number of Convicts,	[illegible]	[illegible]	[illegible]	[illegible]	[illegible]	[illegible]	[illegible]

TABLE XXII.—NUMBER of CONVICTS in each of the CONVICT PRISONS and in the detached party of CONVICTS working in a LOCAL PRISON on the First Day in each Month of the Years 1894 and 1895 (at Lock-up).

PRISONS.	1895.											
	1st Jan.	1st Feb.	1st March.	1st April.	1st May.	1st June.	1st July.	1st Aug.	1st Sept.	1st Oct.	1st Nov.	1st Dec.
Maryborough:—												
Invalids, .	43	40	48	[illegible]	40	43	44	41	40	42	[illegible]	41
Intermediate,	5	6	3	8	9	17	16	19	18	16	14	13
Others, . .	18	13	16	12	11	13	13	9	10	16	8	6
Mountjoy, . .	348	347	347	340	348	[illegible]	[illegible]	[illegible]	[illegible]	[illegible]	[illegible]	316
Cork Male Prison	15	11	11	6	10	14	12	17	16	16	14	16
Total Males, .	427	404	425	404	410	416	409	410	409	394	[illegible]	[illegible]
Grangegorman,	37	37	34	33	36	37	37	[illegible]	35	24	[illegible]	[illegible]
Total M. & F..	464	471	459	[illegible]	447	443	446	436	431	418	415	421

PRISONS.	1894.											
	1st Jan.	1st Feb.	1st March.	1st April.	1st May.	1st June.	1st July.	1st Aug.	1st Sept.	1st Oct.	1st Nov.	1st Dec.
Maryborough:—												
Invalids, .	49	51	51	51	49	47	44	44	41	40	41	39
Intermediate,	6	13	16	11	10	6	7	6	5	6	7	6
Others, . .	6	4	7	8	5	6	6	10	10	9	8	13
Mountjoy, . .	373	378	[illegible]	354	351	[illegible]	[illegible]	354	[illegible]	[illegible]	334	[illegible]
Cork Male, .	–	–	13	13	16	16	14	13	17	16	14	13
Total Males, .	[illegible]	447	444	446	451	437	451	430	427	413	414	411
Grangegorman,	[illegible]	[illegible]	40	41	38	[illegible]	[illegible]	[illegible]	34	34	37	36
Total M. & F..	478	[illegible]	486	486	479	[illegible]	[illegible]	468	466	448	467	447

TABLE XXIV.—CRIMES of CONVICTS committed under fresh sentences of penal servitude during the year ended 31st December, 1896, and of all Convicts in custody on that date.

Crimes.	Number Committed under fresh sentences of penal servitude during year.		No. in custody on 31st Dec., 1896.					
			Maryborough.					
			Invalids.	Imbeciles and others.	Mountjoy.	Cork Male.	Total Males.	Mountjoy Female.
	M.	F.	M.	M.	M.	M.	M.	F.
Accessory after the fact to Murder,	-	-	-	1	-	-	1	-
Aiding and abetting Manslaughter,	1	-	-	-	1	-	1	-
Administering Poison with intent,	-	-	-	-	1	-	1	-
Aiding, &c., to commit Rape,	-	-	-	-	1	-	1	-
Arson,	1	-	-	-	3	-	3	-
Assault, Bodily Harm,	3	-	-	-	3	-	3	-
Assault with intent to Rob,	-	-	-	2	1	-	3	-
Assault and Robbery,	3	-	1	1	14	-	16	3
Attempt to blow up House,	-	-	-	-	1	-	1	-
Attempt to Murder,	-	-	-	3	3	-	4	-
Attempt to know a Girl,	-	-	-	-	1	-	1	-
Attempt to set fire to Dwelling House,	-	-	-	-	1	-	1	-
Base Coin, Having, making, uttering, or intending to utter,	3	-	-	-	6	-	9	-
Bestiality,	-	-	-	1	-	-	1	-
Bigamy,	-	-	-	1	3	-	3	-
Breaking and Entering,	-	-	-	-	3	2	3	-
Burglary,	3	-	-	-	3	-	3	-
Burglary,	6	-	1	-	22	-	24	-
Burglary and Larceny,	-	-	1	-	-	-	1	-
Carnal knowledge of Girl under 13,	1	-	1	-	5	-	6	-
Cattle Stealing,	1	-	-	-	3	-	3	-
Conspiracy to Murder,	-	-	2	-	3	-	3	-
Embezzlement,	-	-	-	-	3	-	3	-
Felony,	1	1	-	-	8	1	10	1
Feloniously Shooting at,	-	-	1	-	-	-	1	-
Forgery,	2	1	-	-	4	-	5	1
Found concealed at night with intent to commit a Felony,	-	-	1	-	-	-	1	-
Having skeleton keys for unlawful purposes,	-	-	1	-	-	-	1	-
Highway Robbery,	4	-	1	-	4	-	6	1
Horse stealing,	-	-	-	-	1	-	1	-
Housebreaking,	7	-	1	2	24	-	27	-
Killing Cattle,	-	-	-	-	1	-	1	-
Larceny, &c.	22	7	9	8	60	-	77	14
Malicious Damage,	1	-	-	-	1	-	1	-
Maliciously throwing stones at a Railway Carriage,	3	-	-	-	2	-	2	-
Manslaughter,	11	1	7	2	42	5	53	3
Murder,	-	1	10	8	14	1	28	8
Obstructing Railway,	-	-	-	-	1	-	1	-
Obtaining Goods and Money by False Pretences,	4	-	-	-	7	-	7	1
Occasioning actual bodily harm,	-	-	-	-	1	-	1	-
Rape,	4	-	-	3	13	-	20	-
Rape and aiding,	-	-	-	-	-	3	3	-
Receiving stolen Goods,	-	-	1	-	-	-	1	-
Receiving and previous conviction,	4	-	-	-	3	-	3	-
Robbery,	2	1	-	-	6	1	6	1
Sheep stealing,	1	-	-	-	2	-	2	-
Shooting at with Intent, &c.,	-	-	-	-	1	-	1	-
Throwing Vitriol, with Intent,	-	1	-	1	1	-	2	1
Unlawful Assembly, &c.	-	-	-	-	1	-	2	-
Unlawfully concealed with Intent,	-	-	-	-	1	-	1	-
Whiteboy Offence,	1	-	-	4	4	3	12	-
Wounding with Intent,	1	-	-	1	3	-	4	-
Wounding and grievous bodily harm,	9	-	-	-	14	1	14	-
Totals,	60	13	37	31	[illegible]	16	[illegible]	30

TABLE XXV.—SENTENCES of CONVICTS committed under fresh sentences of penal servitude during the year ended 31st December, 1895, and of all Convicts in Custody on that date.

Prison.	[illegible]	[illegible]	[illegible]	[illegible]	[illegible]	[illegible]	[illegible]	[illegible]	[illegible]	[illegible]	[illegible]	[illegible]	[illegible]	[illegible]	[illegible]	[illegible]	[illegible]	[illegible]
Convicts committed under fresh sentences of penal servitude during year.																		
Mountjoy, . . m.	41	4	28	–	6	–	1	1	–	–	1	–	–	[illegible]	–	–	–	[illegible]
Grangegorman, f.	7	–	6	–	–	–	–	–	–	–	–	–	–	–	–	–	–	1
Convicts in Custody on 31st December, 1895.																		
Maryborough—Invalids, .	3	–	16	–	4	–	4	–	–	–	1	–	–	4	–	–	–	11
Intermediates, &c.	3	–	[illegible]	–	[illegible]	–	7	–	–	[illegible]	1	–	–	–	–	–	–	4
Mountjoy, . .	97	26	91	–	46	–	[illegible]	[illegible]	–	4	[illegible]	–	2	16	3	1	–	[illegible]
Cork Male, . .	6	–	1	–	3	–	4	–	–	–	–	–	–	1	–	1	–	–
Total Males,	106	29	116	–	61	–	[illegible]	[illegible]	–	7	11	–	3	[illegible]	[illegible]	[illegible]	–	[illegible]
Grangegorman Fem.	11	–	15	–	–	–	1	–	–	–	–	–	–	–	–	–	–	5
Total on 31st Dec., 1895,	[illegible]	29	129	–	64	–	[illegible]	[illegible]	–	7	11	–	3	35	[illegible]	[illegible]	–	[illegible]

TABLE XXVI.—AGES (on Conviction) of CONVICTS committed under fresh sentences of penal servitude during year ended 31st December, 1895, and of all Convicts in Custody on that date; also the number MARRIED and UNMARRIED.

Prison.	16 and under 20 years.	20 and under 25 years.	25 and under 30 years.	30 and under 40 years.	40 and under 50 years.	50 and under 60 years.	60 and under 70 years.	70 and under 80 years.	80 and over.	Total.	Married.	Unmarried.	Not known.
Convicts convicted under fresh sentences of penal servitude during year.													
Mountjoy, . . m.	6	29	36	31	16	5	3	–	–	[illegible]	54	[illegible]	–
Grangegorman, f.	–	3	1	3	1	6	–	–	–	13	4	9	–
Convicts in Custody on 31st December, 1895.													
Maryborough—Invalids, . .	1	8	1	5	9	9	4	7	–	67	30	18	–
Intermediates, &c.	1	8	3	8	5	3	–	–	–	21	9	12	–
Mountjoy, . .	23	63	64	161	44	[illegible]	9	1	–	[illegible]	[illegible]	[illegible]	–
Cork Male, . .	1	4	6	9	1	–	–	–	–	15	8	7	–
Total Males, .	59	73	74	117	61	31	13	6	–	[illegible]	174	279	–
Grangegorman, .	–	3	7	5	4	4	2	1	–	[illegible]	14	14	–
Total on 31st Dec., 1895,	59	76	81	133	65	67	17	7	–	[illegible]	[illegible]	[illegible]	–

Table XXVIII.—Return of Educational Attainments of all Convicts and of Results of Instruction

Prisons.	Information regarding all Prisoners who						
	Average Number of Prisoners under Instruction daily.	Average Number of Hours devoted to Instruction of Prisoners daily.	Condition of Prisoners at beginning of year, or on committal during year.				
			(a) Wholly Ignorant.	(b) Able to Read.	(c) Able to Read and Write.	(d) Able to Read, Write, and Calculate.	Total.
Maryborough, . . .	39	7·25	7	19	17	15	58
Mountjoy, ...	675	4	71	16	60	183	331
Cork, Male, . . .	15	5	-	-	3	13	16
Total Males, . .	112·3	-	78	37	80	202	417
Grangegorman, F., . .	22	4	21	13	5	3	62
Total M. & F. . .	134·3	-	89	50	80	206	479

under Instruction during the Year ended 31st December, 1895, imparted in Prison.

received Instruction in Prison, whether Committed during the Year or before.

Condition of Prisoners at end of year, or on discharge during year.

(a) Number of the Wholly Illiterate,				(b) Number of those able to Read.			(c) Number of those able to Read and Write.		(d) Number of those able to Read, Write, and Calculate.		
[illegible]	[illegible]	[illegible]	Remaining wholly illiterate.	[illegible]	[illegible]	[illegible]	[illegible]	[illegible]	[illegible]	[illegible]	Total.
9	1	6	1	9	2	2	17	6	11	4	[illegible]
-	6	10	3	1	13	6	[illegible]	3	[illegible]	11	[illegible]
-	-	-	-	-	-	-	8	-	26	-	12
3	3	13	5	10	23	6	43	7	[illegible]	15	417
10	6	4	4	6	5	4	4	4	4	3	[illegible]
13	6	22	9	16	[illegible]	8	47	11	[illegible]	17	470

TABLE XXIX.—Cases of SICKNESS, &c., and DISEASES of CONVICTS during the year ended 31st December, 1895.

—	Cork Male.	Maryborough		Mountjoy.	Total Males.	Grangegorman.
		Invalids.	[illegible]			
		M.	M.	M.	M.	F.
Remaining in Hospital on 1st January, 1895,	–	34	1	20	44	7
Admitted to Hospital during year,	6	14	–	251	271	17
Total,	6	48	1	271	316	24
Discharged to their Classes,	5	6	–	231	242	11
Discharged from Prison on Medical grounds,	–	4	–	5	9	4
Do. do. Licence,	–	18	–	–	18	–
Removed to Asylum,	–	3	–	4	7	–
Removed to Invalid Prison,	–	–	–	10	10	–
Do. other Prisons,	–	–	–	–	–	–
Died,	–	3	–	1	4	1
Remaining in Hospital on 31st December, 1895,	–	21	1	17	39	8
Total,	6	48	1	271	326	24
Daily Average Number in Hospital,	·18	29	·1	16·26	44·84	5·02
Number of Extern Patients during year,	15·	363	–	4,430	4,807	304
Daily Average Number of Extern Patients,	4·	1·00	·02	12·3	17·45	·84
Number of cases of each Disease for which Convicts on Sick Register have been treated during year, viz.:—						
Influenza,	–	–	–	48	48	–
Febricula,	–	–	–	21	21	7
Syphilis,	–	–	–	–	–	1
Erysipelas,	–	–	–	8	8	–
Other Parasitic Affections,	–	–	–	–	–	1
Dyspepsia,	–	–	–	1	1	–
Rheumatism,	3	1	–	9	13	1
Phthisis,	–	1	–	–	1	–
Scrofula,	–	–	–	5	5	–
Anaemia,	15	–	–	8	23	–
Old Age,	–	9	–	–	9	–
Apoplexy,	–	1	–	–	1	–
Sciatica,	–	–	–	6	6	–
Epilepsy,	–	–	–	–	–	1
Neuralgia,	10	–	–	3	13	8
Pleurodynia,	7	–	–	–	7	1
Insanity,	–	–	–	6	6	3
Other Diseases of the Brain and Nervous System,	–	1	–	–	1	–
Ulcer of Cornea,	–	–	–	1	1	–
Conjunctivitis,	–	–	–	3	3	–
Other Diseases of Eye or Ear,	2	–	–	1	3	–
Valvular Disease of Heart,	–	4	–	1	5	–
Varicose Veins,	–	3	–	–	3	–
Syncope,	–	–	–	1	1	2
Other Diseases of Circulatory System,	1	–	–	–	1	–
Laryngitis,	–	–	–	1	1	1
Bronchitis,	3	4	–	30	37	5
Bronchitis (chronic),	–	–	–	–	–	1
Pneumonia,	–	–	–	1	1	–

TABLE XXIX.—CASES of SICKNESS, &c., and DISEASES of CONVICTS during the year ended 31st December, 1895—*continued.*

—	Cork Male.	Maryborough: Invalids.	Maryborough: [illegible]	Mountjoy.	Total Males.	Grangegorman.
		M.	M.	M.	M.	F.
Pleurisy,	-	-	-	4	4	-
Congestion of Lungs,	-	-	-	2	2	-
Asthma,	-	1	1	-	2	-
Haemoptysis,	-	-	-	3	3	-
Bronchial Catarrh,	-	-	-	5	5	-
Catarrh,	3	-	-	4	[illegible]	-
Other Diseases of Respiratory System,	-	-	-	-	-	1
Stomatitis,	1	-	-	-	1	-
Gumboil,	1	-	-	6	7	-
Follicular Tonsillitis,	2	-	-	4	6	1
Dyspepsia,	23	1	-	11	[illegible]	-
Haematemesis,	-	-	-	3	[illegible]	-
Gastritis,	-	-	-	1	1	[illegible]
Gastric Ulcer,	-	1	-	-	1	-
Liver Disease,	-	-	-	1	1	-
Colic,	-	-	-	9	9	[illegible]
Peritonitis,	-	-	-	1	1	-
Diarrhoea,	3	-	-	4	7	2
Constipation,	16	4	-	4	24	16
Haemorrhage from Bowels,	-	-	-	1	1	1
Piles,	1	1	-	3	[illegible]	-
Fistula in Ano,	-	-	-	1	[illegible]	-
Other Diseases of Digestive System,	3	-	-	-	3	1
Bronchocele,	-	-	-	-	-	-
Stricture,	-	-	-	1	1	-
Catarrh of Bladder,	-	-	-	-	-	1
Cystitis,	-	-	-	-	-	1
Bright's Disease,	-	1	-	-	1	-
Other Diseases of Urinary System,	-	-	-	-	-	1
Orchitis,	-	-	-	1	1	-
Other Diseases of Generative Organs,	-	-	-	-	-	1
Caries,	-	3	-	-	3	-
Synovitis,	-	-	-	3	3	-
Whitlow,	-	-	-	-	-	-
Lumbago,	6	1	-	4	11	-
Ulcer,	1	1	-	1	[illegible]	-
Psoriasis,	2	-	-	-	[illegible]	-
Boils,	-	-	-	4	4	-
Wounds,	1	-	-	5	6	-
Burns,	-	-	-	1	1	-
Contusions,	1	-	-	-	1	-
Abscess,	-	-	-	4	4	-
Debility,	-	-	-	11	11	[illegible]
Dropsy,	-	1	-	-	1	-
Other Ill-defined Causes,	6	-	-	-	6	1
Observation,	-	-	-	7	7	-
Total,	113	84	1	251	[illegible]	[illegible]

[illegible]

[illegible]	[illegible]	[illegible]	[illegible]	[illegible]	[illegible]		[illegible]	[illegible]	[illegible]	[illegible]	[illegible]	[illegible]	[illegible]
					[illegible]	[illegible]							
[illegible]	[illegible]	[illegible]	[illegible]	[illegible]	[illegible]	[illegible]	[illegible]	[illegible]	[illegible]	[illegible]	[illegible]	[illegible]	[illegible]
[illegible]	[illegible]	[illegible]	[illegible]	[illegible]	[illegible]	[illegible]	[illegible]	[illegible]	[illegible]	[illegible]	[illegible]	[illegible]	[illegible]
[illegible]	[illegible]	[illegible]	[illegible]	[illegible]	[illegible]	[illegible]	[illegible]	[illegible]	[illegible]	[illegible]	[illegible]	[illegible]	[illegible]
[illegible]	[illegible]	[illegible]	[illegible]	[illegible]	[illegible]	[illegible]	[illegible]	[illegible]	[illegible]	[illegible]	[illegible]	[illegible]	[illegible]
[illegible]	[illegible]	[illegible]	[illegible]	[illegible]	[illegible]	[illegible]	[illegible]	[illegible]	[illegible]	[illegible]	[illegible]	[illegible]	[illegible]

[illegible]

TABLE XXXI.—[illegible] of CONVICTS released on MEDICAL GROUNDS during Year ended 31st December, 1886.

[See Paragraph [illegible] of Report of Royal Commission, 1884.]

[illegible]	[illegible]	[illegible]	[illegible]	[illegible]	[illegible]	[illegible]	[illegible]	[illegible]	[illegible]
[illegible]	[illegible]	[illegible]	[illegible]	[illegible]	[illegible]	[illegible]	[illegible]	[illegible]	[illegible]
	[illegible]	[illegible]	[illegible]	[illegible]	[illegible]	[illegible]	[illegible]	[illegible]	[illegible]
	[illegible]	[illegible]	[illegible]	[illegible]	[illegible]	[illegible]	[illegible]	[illegible]	[illegible]
	[illegible]	[illegible]	[illegible]	[illegible]	[illegible]	[illegible]	[illegible]	[illegible]	[illegible]
	[illegible]	[illegible]	[illegible]	[illegible]	[illegible]	[illegible]	[illegible]	[illegible]	[illegible]
	[illegible]	[illegible]	[illegible]	[illegible]	[illegible]	[illegible]	[illegible]	[illegible]	[illegible]
Mountjoy?	[illegible]	[illegible]	[illegible]	[illegible]	[illegible]	[illegible]	[illegible]	[illegible]	[illegible]
	[illegible]	[illegible]	[illegible]	[illegible]	[illegible]	[illegible]	[illegible]	[illegible]	[illegible]
	[illegible]	[illegible]	[illegible]	[illegible]	[illegible]	[illegible]	[illegible]	[illegible]	[illegible]
	[illegible]	[illegible]	[illegible]	[illegible]	[illegible]	[illegible]	[illegible]	[illegible]	[illegible]
Grangegorman?	[illegible]	[illegible]	[illegible]	[illegible]	[illegible]	[illegible]	[illegible]	[illegible]	[illegible]
	[illegible]	[illegible]	[illegible]	[illegible]	[illegible]	[illegible]	[illegible]	[illegible]	[illegible]
	[illegible]	[illegible]	[illegible]	[illegible]	[illegible]	[illegible]	[illegible]	[illegible]	[illegible]
	[illegible]	[illegible]	[illegible]	[illegible]	[illegible]	[illegible]	[illegible]	[illegible]	[illegible]

TABLE XXXII.—PARTICULARS of each case of INSANITY

[See Paragraph 136 of Report of

Prison.	Initials of name.	Sex.	Age on reception (Years).	Education.	Occupation previous to Conviction.	Crime or Charge.	Date of Conviction (if Convicted).	Sentence (if Sentenced).
Maryborough,	D. F.,	M.	[illegible]	Ill.,	Shoemaker,	Larceny and former convictions.	13. 4. 93	7 years P. S.
"	L. K.,	M.	27	R. & W.	Butcher and cattle drover,	Shooting at with intent to do grievous bodily harm.	14. 8. 93	Life P.S.,
Mountjoy,	J. R.,	M.	[illegible]	Ill.,	Labourer,	Manslaughter,	22. 12. 93	15 years P. S.,
"	W. J. M'H.	M.	[illegible]	R. & W.	Plasterer's helper,	Manslaughter,	[illegible]	7 years P. S.,
"	M. C.,	M.	[illegible]	R. & W.	Labourer,	Felony,	[illegible]	10 years P. S.,
"	J. M'D.	M.	46	R. & W.	Labourer,	Housebreaking,	[illegible]	7 years P. S., and [illegible] days of [illegible]
Grangegorman,	B. G.,	F.	[illegible]	Ill.,	Dealer,	Larceny,	[illegible]	5 years P. S.,
"	H. R.,	F.	45	Ill.,	Dealer,	Manslaughter,	[illegible]	5 years P. S.,
"	L. R.,	F.	34	R. & W.	Prostitute,	Malicious injury,	13. 1. 94	5 years P. S.,
"	M. M'E.	F.	[illegible]	R. & W.	Nil,	Larceny from the person, and previous convictions for felony.	27. 1. 94	5 years P. S.,

(amongst Convicts) in Year ended 31st December, 1895.

Royal Commission, 1884.]

Date of Reception.	Mental Condition on Reception.	Whether previously Insane.	Length of imprisonment previous to first symptoms of Insanity (in cases originating in Prison).	Form of Insanity.	Termination of Case.				
					Recovered in Prison.	Removed to Asylum.		Died in Prison until date.	Remaining in Prison.
						Name of Asylum.	Date of Removal.		
[illegible]	Good, .	No, .	1 year and 13½ months.	Delusional mania.	–	Dundrum, .	4. 4. 95	–	–
[illegible]	Good, .	No, .	13 years. This man appeared to be always more or less eccentric.	Delusional mania.	–	Dundrum, .	7. 10. 95	–	–
6. 7. 95	Good, .	No record,	1 year, .	Suicidal mania.	–	Dundrum, .	11. 5. 95	–	–
20. 4. 94	Good, .	No record,	1 month, .	Suicidal mania.	–	Dundrum, .	9. 7. 95	–	–
[illegible]	Good, .	Yes, .	7 years and 6 months.	Suicidal mania.	–	Dundrum, .	[illegible]	–	–
[illegible]	Good, .	No record,	3 years and 10 months	Mania,	–	Dundrum, .	[illegible]	–	–
[illegible] 12. 94	Unsound,	Yes, .	—	Mania, .	–	Dundrum, .	14. 6. 95	–	–
18. 1. 92	Unsound,	Not known,	—	Sub-acute mania.	–	Dundrum, .	6. 4. 95	–	–
1. 12. 94	Unsound,	Yes, .	—	Recurrent mania.	–	Dundrum, .	27. 1. 95	–	–
15. 1. 94	Unsound,	Yes, .	—	Recurrent mania.	–	Dundrum, .	27. 7. 95	–	–

TABLE XXXIV.—WORKS of RECONSTRUCTION, REPAIRS, &c., by Contract and by Prison Labour, during year ended 31st December, 1895.

CONVICT PRISONS.

Prison.	Labour. (Contract or Prison).	Detail of Works.
Maryborough, .	Contract,	Shortened pump rods and rising main pipe of new deep spring well pump at back of prison, fixed a new set of valves in same and erected a new pedestal for pumping gear.
Do., . . .	Prison, .	Built with concrete two new warders' cottages, roofed, slated, rendered, and plastered same, gutters and rain-water pipes fixed, sashes glazed and fixed, doors trimmings, and staircase prepared and fixed, kitchen ranges, grates, and mantels set, built pavilion and ancillaries for same; repaired hot air engines, and auxiliary pumps in laundry; whitewashed and painted the two cottages in occupation; painted cell doors, staircases, and corridors of Prison; whitewashed cells and inside walls of prison and officers' quarters; repaired the lead gutters and valleys of roofs of prison, Governor's house, and Hospital, regulated flushing valves of "A" Yard, "B" and "C" Prisons.
Mountjoy, . .	Contract,	Two lightning conductors fixed up to large chimney stacks and air shafts.
Do., . .	Prison, .	One sentry box and 6 wheelbarrows made for Waterford prison; 4 closet seats made for Armagh prison; 3 closet seats made for Spike Island prison; repairs to boilers, heating pipes, &c., in the prison hospital, laundry, baths, and cookhouses, and including repairs to the ovens, fire bars, &c.; repairs to roofs of convict and local prisons, and roof lights repaired and painted; general repairs to buildings, boundary walls, &c., including brick and stonework, woodwork, plumbing, gasfitting, locks, gates, &c.; the walls of cells, corridors, &c., limewhitened, and woodwork and ironwork painted; 12 sashes for cell windows fitted with wrought-iron ventilating flaps; small enclosure with sash door, check gate, &c.; 1 closet seat, 4 wood-drying tables, and 6 wheelbarrows, made for Kilmainham prison; wire trellis, with G.B. standards, prepared and fixed round galleries of new hall at Grangegorman prison, with all necessary clips, bolts, and holdfasts; shelving with drawers for surgery prepared for Grangegorman prison; chapel fittings for Protestant chapel at Londonderry prepared; 12 mat-making frames, and 12 coal boxes, also made for Londonderry prison; 6 new doors, with hinges, &c., and 4 wheelbarrows made for Sligo prison; 1 bookcase and 2 closet seats made for Clonmel prison; 22 warders' cottages continued; joinery work, plastering, tiling of floors, plumbing work to W.C's., scullery, &c., and gasfitting finished, and painting in progress; the boundary walls to yards, &c., are being built, and roads, channels, &c., formed; wire protection netting, with G.B. standards, prepared and fixed round galleries of B and C divisions, and fixed with clips, bolts, holdfasts, &c.; new hot water cistern and boiler, fitted up in Governor's house to replace old ones; staircases papered and ceilings cleaned, basement whitened and woodwork painted; new hot water cistern fitted up in hospital, and boiler repaired and reset; 8 warders' cottages cleaned, whitened, and painted; ovens in bakery repaired, including tiling, fire bars, &c.
Grangegorman, .	Contract,	Nil.
Do., . .	Prison, .	Ceilings of passages and cells limewashed and walls coloured; doors and windows painted; all necessary repairs to carpentry, plumbing, gasfitting, bellhanging, and glazing executed in convict division.

TABLE XXXV.—SHOWING employment of Convicts and estimated value of their Earnings.

CORK MALE PRISON.

No. 1.—VALUE of the Labour of Convicts (as per measured work) for the year ended 31st March, 1896.

Work.	Daily Average (working days).	No. of Days.		Rate per day earned (see Summary).	Amount.
				d.	£ s. d.
Prison Buildings, . . .	13·[illegible]	–	4,189	30·05	545 18 7
NON-EFFECTIVE.					
Sick, ...	·237	73	–	–	
Under Punishment, . . .	·026	8	–	–	
Not told off to parties, . .	·557	163	310	–	
		Working days.			
	14·4[illegible]	in [illegible]	4,499	18·93	545 18 7

No. 2.—SUMMARY of Earnings of the various Trades or Parties for the year ended 31st March, 1896.

No. of Party.	Employment.	No. of Days.	Average Earnings per Convict per Day as measured and valued.	Amount.
			d.	£ s. d.
	PRISON BUILDINGS.			
–	Labourers, ...	1,930	16	129 1 4
–	Scaffolding, ...	179	24	23 18 0
–	Carpentering, ...	1,189	24	118 18 0
–	Masons, ...	617	24	64 14 0
–	Painting, ...	203	20·0	16 9 8
–	Whitewashing, ...	18	12	0 18 0
–	Plastering, ...	246	24	24 17 0
	Total, ...	4,189	29·05	545 18 7

TABLE XXXV.—SHOWING employment of Convicts and estimated value of their Earnings—*continued.*

MARYBOROUGH CONVICT PRISON.

No. 1.—VALUE of the Labour of Convicts (as per measured work) for the year ended 31st March, 1896.

Work.	Daily Average (Working Days).	Number of Days.		Rate per day earned (see Summary).	Amount.
				d.	£ s. d.
Manufactory,	7·11	2,161	–	17·	168 1 5
Prison Buildings,	7·6	2,304	–	16·81	163 0 0
	14·71	–	4,465	16·9	[illegible]
Prison Employment,	30·7	–	9,393	13·	464 10 0
Totals,	45·41	–	13,757	14·7	[illegible] 1 5
NON-EFFECTIVE.					
Under Punishment,	·11	–	36	–	—
Exempt from Labour on Medical grounds,	15·15	–	5,397	–	—
Grand Totals,	60· × 303 =		19,194	[illegible]	[illegible] 1 5

No. 2.—SUMMARY of Earnings of the various Trades or Parties, for the year ended 31st March, 1896.

No. of Party.	Employment.	No. of Days.	Average Earnings per Convict per Day as measured and valued.	Amount.
			d.	£ s. d.
	MANUFACTORY.			
–	Tailoring,	1,[illegible]	17·	121 15 6
–	Shoemaking,	631	16·	42 5 1
		2,161	17·	168 1 5
	PRISON BUILDINGS.			
–	Carpenters,	362	24·	36 4 0
–	Masons and Plasterers,	402	24·	40 4 0
–	Labourers,	1,540	14·	90 0 0
		2,304	16·81	163 0 0
	PRISON EMPLOYMENT.			
–	Labourers,	1,010	18·	75 15 0
–	Gardening,	1,716	13·	93 19 0
–	Cleaning Prison,	2,191	13·	119 1 0
–	Repairing Clothing and Bedding,	2,278	13·	123 18 0
–	Washing Clothing and Bedding,	668	13·	36 3 8
–	Cooking,	802	13·	43 9 0
		9,393	13·	464 10 0

TABLE XXXV.—SHOWING employment of Convicts and estimated value of their Earnings—*continued.*

MOUNTJOY CONVICT PRISON.

No. 1.—VALUE of the Labour of Convicts (as per measured work), for the year ended 31st March, 1896.

Work.	Daily Average (working days.)	No. of Days.		Rate per day earned (see Summary).	Amount.		
				d.	£	s.	d.
Manufactory,	180·620	56,820·167	-	21·29	2,996	5	1
Prison Buildings,	55·835	19,603·484	79,523·631	19·65	1,546	6	10
					4,542	9	11
Prison Employment,	38·45	-	11,616·33	19·57	848	17	7
Totals,	300·934	-	91,145·969	13·93	5,391	7	6
NON-EFFECTIVE.							
Sick,	15·863	4,616·755	-	-			
Under punishment,	1·368	417·855	-	-			
Not told off to parties,	2·865	875·847		-			
			6,[illegible]·020				
		Working days.					
Grand Totals,	320·776	× 305 =	97,[illegible]	17·36	5,391	7	6

No. 2.—SUMMARY of Earnings of the various Trades or Parties, for the year ended 31st March, 1896.

No. of Party.	Employment.	No. of Days.	Average Earnings per Convict per Day as measured and valued.	Amount.		
	MANUFACTORY.		d.	£	s.	d.
-	Tailoring,	15,[illegible]·760	25·5	1,[illegible]	17	0
-	Shoemaking,	12,[illegible]·183	10·5	545	15	0
-	Oakum Picking,	1,[illegible]·736	·39	2	1	10
-	Matmaking,	12,[illegible]·760	8·37	467	9	6
-	Baking,	1,780·[illegible]	25·6	191	9	7
-	Carpentering,	1,[illegible]·136	26·	146	14	3
-	Cutting Firewood,	5,762·12	7·36	176	15	6
-	Tinsmithing,	473·154	26·	47	16	0
		50,[illegible]·187	13·90	2,996	8	1
	PRISON BUILDINGS.					
-	Labouring,	8,[illegible]·775	16·	542	17	6
-	Smithing,	1,[illegible]·282	24·	143	4	7
-	Carpentering,	4,[illegible]·341	26·	483	6	5
-	Masons,	[illegible]·[illegible]	25·	81	15	10
-	Painting,	1,[illegible]·78	20·6	112	17	6
-	Whitewashing,	[illegible]·[illegible]	18·	6	9	5
-	Plastering,	1,767·[illegible]	24·	176	14	10
		19,603·484	17·88	1,546	6	10
	PRISON EMPLOYMENT.					
-	Cleaning,	6,104·[illegible]	17·	262	16	5
-	Store Porters,	1,[illegible]·864	12·	57	15	10
-	Stokers,	[illegible]·[illegible]	16·	15	13	4
-	Cooks,	1,[illegible]·[illegible]	16·4	167	16	0
-	Washing,	2,[illegible]·[illegible]	18·	148	7	11
-	Bookbinding,	[illegible]·[illegible]	26·	84	16	5
		15,[illegible]·[illegible]	13·37	846	17	7

TABLE XXXV.—SHOWING employment of Convicts and estimated value of their Earnings—*continued.*

GRANGEGORMAN CONVICT PRISON.

No. 1.—VALUE of the Labour of Convicts (as per measured work) for the year ended 31st March, 1896.

Work.	Daily Average (working days).	No. of Days.		Rate per day earned (see Summary).	Amount.
				d.	£ s. d.
Manufactory, . . .	13·27	4,717·61	–	10·	154 18 2
Prison employment, . .	3·90	1,896·70	–	13·36	102 18 8
Totals, . .	21·17	–	6,614·31	10·84	257 16 10
NON-EFFECTIVE.					
Punishment, . . .	·07	21·21	–	–	—
Sick in Cells, &c., . .	·76	230·22	–	–	—
Hospital, ...	5·80	1,830·11	–	–	—
		Working days.	1,381·63	Average earnings.	
Grand Totals, .	27·24	[illegible] –	8,296·15	8·71	257 16 10

No. 2.—SUMMARY of the Earnings of the various Trades or Parties, for the year ended 31st March, 1896.

No. of Party.	Employment.	No. of Days.	Average Earnings per Convict per Day as measured and valued.	Amount.
	MANUFACTORY.		d.	£ s. d.
–	Knitting and Needlewomen. . . .	4,717·61	10	154 18 2
	PRISON EMPLOYMENT.			
–	Cooking for Prisoners, . . .	1,103·85	22·	100 11 9
–	Washing Prisoners' Clothing, . .	487·82	13·2	22 1 4
–	Cleaning Prison, ...	1,302·93	10·5	43 17 7
		2,896·70	14·28	102 10 8

Daily Average Number of Convicts in Custody during the Year, . . . 22·31

Per-centage on Prison Population Working, ... 74·20

Do. do. do. Sick, &c., ... 21·33

Do. do. do. in Punishment, ... ·25

APPENDIX.

PART IV.

REGISTRATION OF HABITUAL CRIMINALS, &c.

TABLES.

[illegible]

TABLE XXXVII.—NUMBER of queries as to Prisoners in Custody awaiting Trial, received from Prisons and Police during each of the following years, showing the per-centage known:—

YEAR.	Queries received from.		Per-centage known.	
	Prisons.	Police.	Prisons.	Police.
1870a,	–	–	–	–
1871b,	47	27	81·9	15·
1872,	90	40	85·56	25·
1873,	151	24	37·08	46·
1874,	133	42	40·8	35·08
1875,	164	32	53·64	15·62
1876,	130	25	26·15	8·
1877,	92	24	19·56	29·
1878,	73	20	26·	25·
1879,	57	35	21·	8·6
1880,	153	75	51·9	1·07
1880–81,	148	62	60·8	6·
1881–82,	140	13	79·3	7·7
1882–83,	99	15	81·8	6·6
1883–84,	86	3	62·3	–
1884–85,	[illegible]	6	63·7	50·
1885–86,	[illegible]	9	95·	11·
1886–87,	101	5	87·	40·
1887–88,	94	2	91·5	100·
1888–89,	91	–	94·6	–
1889–90,	69	1	96·5	·
1890–91,	98	5	96·	20·
1891–92,	75	–	98·0	·
1892–93,	74	5	94·6	·60
1893–94,	71	1	97·	–
1894–95,	99	–	97·9	–
1895,	66	–	93·4	–

a. No record kept. b. Commencing August, 1871.

TABLE XXXVIII.—NUMBER of habitual criminals registered in:

Year.	No.	Year.	No.
1870,	907	1883–84,	164
1871,	1,058	1884–85,	178
1872,	840	1885–86,	208
1873,	1,118	1886–87,	210
1874,	1,069	1887–88,	155
1875,	980	1888–89,	160
1876,	964	1889–90,	131
1877,	609	1890–91,	183
1878,	372	1891–92,	144
1879,	305	1892–93,	140
1880–81*,	285	1893–94,	125
1881–82,	224	1894–95,	181
1882–83,	169	1895,	169

* From 1st January, 1880, to 31st March, 1881.

APPENDIX.

PART V.

EXPENDITURE—CONVICT AND LOCAL PRISONS
(Inclusive of Bridewells).

TABLE

showing

THE EXPENDITURE UNDER HEADS OF SERVICE

In the Year ended 31st March, 1896.

Table XXXIX.—EXPENDITURE—CONVICT AND

Return showing the Expenditure under Heads

Heads of Service.	Totals.	Mountjoy.
Daily average number of prisoners (including Minor Prisons and Bridewells).	M. 7,646 / F. 816	M. 674
Cost of Staff.	£ s. d.	£ s. d.
Pay and allowances of officers, including uniforms, &c.,	49,445 5 6	13,478 12 4
Average annual charge per prisoner,	18 12 1	21 13 4
Maintenance of Prisoners.		
Victualling for prisoners,	14,665 8 8	3,649 5 3
Clothing for prisoners,	3,216 6 5	642 16 7
Medicines, surgical instruments, &c.,	409 8 11	176 9 8
Soap, scouring and cleaning articles,	678 17 10	143 14 4
Fuel, light, and water,	3,466 11 1	2,715 7 1
Total expenses of Maintenance,	22,707 7 8	7,409 12 3
Average annual charge per prisoner,	10 16 6	12 13 11
Other Expenses.		
Bedding for prisoners,	827 10 4	181 7 6
Gratuities to prisoners,	944 16 8	986 5 10
Furniture, kitchen utensils, crockery, &c.	888 18 6	311 10 6
Rent,	475 10 1	6 1 6
Ordinary repairs of buildings,	3,441 16 10	309 8 11
Incidental expenses,	1,176 2 9	110 16 8
Total of other Expenses,	7,127 17 4	985 6 7
Average annual charge per prisoner,	3 16 11	1 13 5
Gross Total Expenses for the Year.		
Aggregate,	94,282 11 4	21,396 17 1
Per prisoner,	37 4 8	34 10 7

Heads of Service.	Armagh.	Belfast.	Castlebar.
Daily average number of prisoners (including Minor Prisons and Bridewells).	M. 60 / F. 29	M. 260 / F. 141	M. 45 / F. 4
Cost of Staff.	£ s. d.	£ s. d.	£ s. d.
Pay and allowances of officers, including uniforms, &c.	1,780 5 1	4,320 0 8	1,169 12 4
Average annual charge per prisoner,	19 4 8	10 11 11	23 16 0
Maintenance of Prisoners.			
Victualling for prisoners,	180 11 4	2,647 10 11	267 17 6
Clothing for prisoners,	79 14 9	675 0 1	46 19 6
Medicines, surgical instruments, &c.,	34 7 6	41 14 8	3 6 7
Soap, scouring and cleaning articles,	75 7 5	101 15 1	12 11 3
Fuel, light, and water,	253 3 6	617 0 5	323 1 7
Total expenses of Maintenance,	628 13 4	3,378 13 5	655 1 7
Average annual charge per prisoner,	9 0 4	6 6 9	15 1 10
Other Expenses.			
Bedding for prisoners,	91 5 4	61 5 5	6 1 5
Gratuities to prisoners,	10 6 0	118 11 5	4 19 0
Furniture, kitchen utensils, crockery, &c.,	19 4 1	64 8 6	12 11 3
Rent,	—	9 14 8	—
Ordinary repairs of buildings,	196 9 6	717 10 2	86 4 1
Incidental expenses,	40 1 11	50 7 8	26 6 4
Total of other Expenses,	364 9 1	437 10 3	40 5 9
Average annual charge per prisoner,	3 6 11	1 8 11	3 15 7
Gross Total Expenses for the Year.			
Aggregate,	2,804 7 6	8,136 5 7	1,868 0 1
Per prisoner,	33 16 6	29 7 8	61 6 2

* The medicines for Grangegorman Prison were supplied

LOCAL PRISONS (inclusive of Bridewells).

of Service, in the year ended 31st March, 1896.

Grangegorman.	Maryborough.	Heads of Service.
F. 104	M. 64	Daily average number of prisoners (including Minor Prisons and Bridewells).
£ s. d.	£ s. d.	Cost of Staff.
2,253 9 8	2,465 5 0	Pay and allowances of officers, including uniforms, &c.
14 17 0	37 11 8	Average annual charge per prisoner.
		Maintenance of Prisoners.
2,084 8 1	774 1 10	Victualling for prisoners.
114 7 9	150 4 10	Clothing for prisoners.
31 8 11*	32 15 6	Medicines, surgical instruments, &c.
48 11 10	17 13 8	Soap, scouring and cleaning articles.
749 1 9	423 10 4	Fuel, light, and water.
3,029 5 11	1,384 7 1	Total expenses of Maintenance.
9 15 6	21 4 6	Average annual charge per prisoner.
		Other Expenses.
31 0 6	26 4 2	Bedding for prisoners.
71 18 7	175 8 2	Gratuities to prisoners.
70 13 9	52 7 0	Furniture, kitchen utensils, crockery, &c.
—	—	Rent.
371 16 8	209 1 7	Ordinary repairs of buildings.
56 10 5	71 18 9	Incidental expenses.
603 16 11	536 10 6	Total of other Expenses.
7 16 0	7 18 5	Average annual charge per prisoner.
		Gross Total Expenses for the Year.
5,614 7 10	4,788 11 9	Aggregate.
54 10 6	68 13 11	Per prisoner.

Clonmel.	Cork, Male.	Cork, Female.	Heads of Service.
M. 40	M. 188	F. 67	Daily average number of prisoners (including Minor Prisons and Bridewells).
£ s. d.	£ s. d.	£ s. d.	Cost of Staff.
1,490 8 2	2,506 14 6	1,123 6 8	Pay and allowances of officers, including uniforms, &c.
35 0 11	13 13 7	19 9 4	Average annual charge per prisoner.
			Maintenance of Prisoners.
385 15 0	940 6 8	433 12 4	Victualling for prisoners.
71 14 1	226 1 6	79 7 6	Clothing for prisoners.
12 0 10	34 13 5	30 10 9	Medicines, surgical instruments, &c.
79 15 10	84 15 7	25 4 6	Soap, scouring and cleaning articles.
180 14 5	627 9 3	249 0 6	Fuel, light, and water.
730 14 1	1,854 3 8	816 14 6	Total expenses of Maintenance.
10 14 5	7 15 8	9 7 9	Average annual charge per prisoner.
			Other Expenses.
9 15 6	27 6 7	21 10 5	Bedding for prisoners.
84 4 8	48 16 4	15 16 11	Gratuities to prisoners.
14 6 9	64 17 4	33 5 10	Furniture, kitchen utensils, crockery, &c.
129 2 0	—	40 0 0	Rent.
44 15 3	170 17 11	124 0 4	Ordinary repairs of buildings.
89 16 1	60 12 9	74 6 8	Incidental expenses.
371 19 7	373 10 11	345 1 8	Total of other Expenses.
8 16 10	1 16 2	5 10 4	Average annual charge per prisoner.
			Gross Total Expenses for the Year.
2,082 0 10	4,834 10 8	2,285 0 1	Aggregate.
67 14 2	25 7 3	35 7 7	Per prisoner.

at Mountjoy Prison and supplied from that establishment, up to 30th June, 1895.

Table XXXIX.—Convict and Local

Return showing the Expenditure under Heads

Heads of Service	Dundalk.	Galway.	Kilkenny.
Daily average number of prisoners (including Minor Prisons and Bridewells).	m. 43, f. 2	m. 97, f. 14	m. 93
Cost of Staff.	£ s. d.	£ s. d.	£ s. d.
Pay and allowances of officers, including uniforms, &c.	1,422 9 10	1,420 0 9	1,418 18 1
Average annual charge per prisoner,	29 10 4	23 8 4	14 18 3
Maintenance of Prisoners.			
Victualling for prisoners,	297 8 0	548 16 5	427 0 4
Clothing for prisoners,	68 4 1	78 7 8	40 3 7
Medicines, surgical instruments, &c.,	16 11 0	14 10 3	11 16 7
Soap, scouring and cleaning articles,	81 4 11	15 3 11	31 4 11
Fuel, light, and water,	246 10 11	177 0 7	134 10 4
Total expenses of Maintenance,	693 7 5	778 6 8	631 4 11
Average annual charge per prisoner,	16 12 9	11 4 9	6 5 1
Other Expenses.			
Bedding for prisoners,	94 11 10	0 1 4	10 0 3
Gratuities to prisoners,	11 14 0	10 8 5	17 10 7
Furniture, kitchen utensils, crockery, &c.,	17 5 7	73 18 7	31 13 11
Rent,	44 11 0	—	—
Ordinary repairs of buildings,	178 13 0	71 1 8	78 9 7
Incidental expenses,	11 16 8	41 5 8	99 17 3
Total of other Expenses,	388 0 0	1[illegible] 2 10	188 0 7
Average annual charge per prisoner,	9 7 4	7 10 11	2 0 0
Gross Total Expense for the Year.			
Aggregate,	2,634 6 5	2,143 9 8	2,160 3 10
Per prisoner,	46 5 5	37 8 5	26 13 4

Heads of Service.	Sligo.	Tralee.
Daily average number of prisoners (including Minor Prisons and Bridewells).	m. 44, f. 12	m. 47, f. 6
Cost of Staff.	£ s. d.	£ s. d.
Pay and allowances of officers, including uniforms, &c.	2,216 19 0	1,175 4 9
Average annual charge per prisoner,	41 5 1	24 8 10
Maintenance of Prisoners.		
Victualling for prisoners,	324 8 9	280 8 11
Clothing for prisoners,	70 15 1	50 10 8
Medicines, surgical instruments, &c.,	34 8 9	13 4 0
Soap, scouring and cleaning articles,	17 6 8	11 8 4
Fuel, light, and water,	297 5 10	103 11 11
Total expenses of Maintenance,	636 14 1	487 17 4
Average annual charge per prisoner,	11 4 0	10 3 8
Other Expenses.		
Bedding for prisoners,	30 8 0	0 14 6
Gratuities to prisoners,	32 10 11	19 4 4
Furniture, kitchen utensils, crockery, &c.,	51 10 8	14 8 6
Rent,	41 13 10	48 0 0
Ordinary repairs of buildings,	176 4 10	63 18 4
Incidental expenses,	34 8 7	88 17 2
Total of other Expenses,	247 10 2	148 17 11
Average annual charge per prisoner,	4 0 0	3 0 0
Gross Total Expense for the Year.		
Aggregate,	3,250 7 8	1,808 0 1
Per prisoner,	58 6 10	37 13 3

PRISONS (inclusive of Bridewells)—*continued.*

of Service, in the year ended 31st March, 1891—*continued.*

Kilmainham.	Limerick, Male.	Limerick Female.	Londonderry.	HEADS OF SERVICE.
M. 247	M. 89	F. 47	M. 76, F. 13	Daily average number of prisoners (including Minor Prisons and Bridewells).
£ s. d.	£ s. d.	£ s. d.	£ s. d.	COST OF STAFF.
2,335 11 2	1,902 0 6	793 8 8	2,434 7 6	Pay and allowances of officers, including uniforms, &c.
15 17 9	19 16 2	16 8 10	31 10 6	Average annual charge per prisoner.
				MAINTENANCE OF PRISONERS.
624 3 9	579 16 3	278 16 0	616 1 10	Victualling for prisoners.
163 4 11	107 13 3	36 8 6	111 15 6	Clothing for prisoners.
78 16 10	14 0 9	8 17 0	10 13 6	Medicine, surgical instruments, &c.
34 6 2	59 12 4	9 0 9	83 10 10	Soap, scouring and cleaning articles.
313 9 6	314 11 7	157 0 5	440 10 10	Fuel, light, and water.
1,159 0 9	1,086 2 6	482 16 0	2,277 17 5	Total expenses of Maintenance.
7 14 10	16 3 0	9 13 1	11 14 6	Average annual charge per prisoner.
				OTHER EXPENSES.
17 12 0	9 5 9	1 9 6	25 2 7	Bedding for prisoners.
57 4 1	61 14 5	6 7 0	61 10 7	Gratuities to prisoners.
51 19 2	78 10 6	10 11 4	41 0 6	Furniture, kitchen utensils, crockery, &c.
7 5 4	—	—	—	Rent.
219 11 4	217 4 6	183 7 8	215 16 2	Ordinary repairs of buildings.
111 17 6	47 9 6	36 1 11	61 6 6	Incidental expenses.
465 7 5	426 7 1	246 8 8	421 16 3	Total of other Expenses.
3 0 7	4 4 11	5 3 8	3 17 4	Average annual charge per prisoner.
				GROSS TOTAL EXPENSES FOR THE YEAR.
5,619 14 3	3,406 9 11	1,523 14 9	4,141 13 8	Aggregate.
22 13 7	38 7 0	32 6 8	56 2 6	Per prisoner.

Tullamore.	Waterford.	Wexford.	HEADS OF SERVICE.
M. 76, F. 10	M. 43, F. 75	M. 24, F. 6	Daily average number of prisoners (including Minor Prisons and Bridewells).
£ s. d.	£ s. d.	£ s. d.	COST OF STAFF.
1,403 10 4	1,374 4 1	1,121 8 4	Pay and allowances of officers, including uniforms, &c.
18 5 0	17 13 4	37 14 1	Average annual charge per prisoner.
			MAINTENANCE OF PRISONERS.
574 15 3	545 14 6	371 10 2	Victualling for prisoners.
137 10 5	99 17 2	51 1 0	Clothing for prisoners.
4 11 7	16 14 8	5 7 1	Medicine, surgical instruments, &c.
96 14 3	73 6 1	18 3 9	Soap, scouring and cleaning articles.
270 18 0	194 16 10	113 19 11	Fuel, light, and water.
1,083 16 8	819 5 10	480 16 4	Total expenses of Maintenance.
26 18 4	10 18 1	11 7 3	Average annual charge per prisoner.
			OTHER EXPENSES.
10 11 5	25 14 11	9 9 4	Bedding for prisoners.
65 18 6	17 0 11	7 14 5	Gratuities to prisoners.
58 5 4	19 11 7	16 7 4	Furniture, kitchen utensils, crockery, &c.
—	—	207 11 0	Rent.
199 0 2	300 3 6	22 19 9	Ordinary repairs of buildings.
74 10 2	91 3 4	20 15 8	Incidental expenses.
408 6 11	478 9 7	285 10 4	Total of other Expenses.
8 14 9	3 8 7	9 10 4	Average annual charge per prisoner.
			GROSS TOTAL EXPENSES FOR THE YEAR.
2,771 10 5	2,569 17 8	1,822 5 8	Aggregate.
64 1 4	30 8 8	60 15 7	Per prisoner.

www.ingramcontent.com/pod-product-compliance
Lightning Source LLC
Chambersburg PA
CBHW020104170426
43199CB00009B/383
* 9 7 8 3 7 4 2 8 1 0 1 9 9 *